Women Who Win Publishing

Fulfill your Dream of being a Published Author with a leader in Women's Inspirational Publishing. At **Women Who Win Publishing** we are **dedicated to publishing** the **stories, wisdom and insights** of women like **YOU** and to publish content that empowers, inspires and uplifts.   Elizabeth believes that when a woman discovers her true purpose, believes in herself, and takes action to move forward that is when she will walk into her destiny.

To learn about our current book project:
www.WomenWhoWin.us

Girl, Get Your Fight Back

Define Yourself, Your Relationships & Your Money
An Anthology

Elizabeth Felder

Cindy
love
Jeman :)

Girl, Get Your Fight Back

Define Yourself, Your Relationships & Your Money
An Anthology

Elizabeth Felder

Table of Contents

About the Publisher

Elizabeth Felder is a Publisher, Entrepreneur, and Inspirational Speaker dedicated to providing a venue for women to share their stories and wisdom. Her desire to empower women gave rise to Women Who Win Publishing, a series of print and digital inspirational anthologies for women and by women.

Elizabeth readily draws upon her extensive experience from over 20 years in corporate law, real estate and entrepreneurship. She is an over-comer of the adversity of domestic abuse, abandonment, bankruptcy, divorce and homelessness.

As a Speaker, Elizabeth has been invited to share her story with audiences, colleges, women's groups, and thereby providing women with tools and tips to connect to their purpose and passion.

In 2005, Elizabeth launched UnStoppable, LLC, a full-service empowerment firm providing financial literacy and empowerment training. In addition, Elizabeth founded the UnStoppable Women & Teens, an organization that helps low income youth and women learn to rebuild their lives and empower them for greatness.

Elizabeth believes that when women speak up, they change History. She has created a powerful platform for connecting women, igniting passions and creating breakthroughs. Her mission is to "Empower Women to Empower the World" exemplifies our commitment to making the world a better place through women's passion and purpose. Her programs enhance, empower, educate and expand women's lives to assist them in discovering their fullest potential, unleash their passion and overcome obstacles to achieve dreams and goals in their life.

To learn more about Elizabeth visit her on the web at www.WomenWhoWin.us

Girl, Get Your Fight Back

Have you ever been through a trial you believed and thought you would never get through? Did you feel disconnected, depressed, angry, lonely, misunderstood and perhaps you even felt suicidal? Every woman has faced the storms of life and may have dealt with many, if not all, of these emotions. Don't be discouraged, because there is hope! There is a power in you, that you can draw upon that will strengthen you to persevere and get your fight back even after life knocks you down.

I'd like to introduce you to an extraordinary group of ladies who have removed their masks and stepped forward to share their stories, wisdom, and life experiences. Their intent is to inspire you and other women to BELIEVE the power is within to overcome obstacles, circumstances, challenges, negative situations and an unpleasant past to go on and live as a Woman – "Who Got Her Fight Back".

With the tools and knowledge in this book, you will realize that your past does not define your future, but your actions do! We hope this book challenges you to know all things are possible with God regardless of your situation. Are you ready to move on and move forward? This book is for women who have decided to do something about their present, who are tired of talking the talk and not walking the walk.

If you're leading an unfulfilled life, then it's time to awaken to your seeds of greatness because regardless of what anyone has told you, there is enormity in you. When you realize that deep within immensity is aching to be expressed, you will become inspired; therefore, when you act upon that greatness, you become great. The earth needs you and your family needs you. Perhaps those around you need to be encouraged too. Who knows, you may be the individual to point the way, and show them all things are possible.

As you read each woman's story, you will begin your own journey to wholeness. Now - let's go ......

Coach Elizabeth Felder
Women Who Win Publishing
President of UnStoppable Women Who Win Network

Inspirational Stories of Women Who Got Their Fight Back

Define
Yourself

From Crisis To Blessing
by Tamara Elizabeth

"Out of every crisis comes the chance to be reborn."
— Nena O'Neil

On the journey of life, each of us from time to time experience crisis from different life changing events and transitions. A crisis can be defined as a particular stage in a sequence of events, which is expected to lead to an unstable or very dangerous situation affecting an individual, group, community or whole society. It is known as a turning point. We travel through most crisis with as much skill and ease as the tools we have been given. When I look back over the last fifty years of my life there were many occasions which I had to step up to the plate and thus these events have somehow carved out the woman I am today. I've worn many hats, in fact enough to fill my own millinery shop. Each role has led me to a series of challenging transitions, several lessons, and celebrated times.

My moment of having the fight knocked out of me was when I found out that my beloved mother had passed. She died this past September and although I knew she was ill with pancreatic cancer. I was not prepared for the news which I would receive on that day. For the moment; however, mother was rallying in strength and ready to tackle the monster of cancer and was geared up to finally leave the hospital. Just as her journey looked as if she should recover, she died instantly of a massive brain aneurism.

The loss of a parent at any age is devastating. This person —your mother- represents the beacon, blinking faithfully in all storms of life to help guide you through your turbulences. When that persevering unrelenting light goes out, there is a deep void and a feeling of loss, but with time heals. However, at the very moment of conception it burns with pain; a pain not possible to overcome anytime soon. In my circumstance there was an added villain to the mixture. The most disappointing thing about the situation is my mom passed on without us reconciling the years of non-communication. We were estranged right to the very end. Our "falling out" happened for reasons I now recognize, I will never know. Perhaps the basis for the **unreconciliation** were not as important as the lessons I was about to learn.

Considering the crisis in my life, this one is paramount. It has ushered me into the personal discovery of who I am and definitely what I'm made of. I tried without success for over a year to make amends with my mother and to accept my part in the conflict between the two of us. Unfortunately, she would not budge in the process of discovering our differences and celebrating them, learning what we needed from each other, and then letting go. She went on to rest peacefully without a word to me. The silence of the fact was deafening to say the least. As I made arrangements to fly to be with my father, during this moment, I was suddenly engulfed with so much disappointment and hurt that I fell to my knees with tears. I had to release the penned up emotions, so my wounds could heal. Through the tears and the sorrow, I took a great deal of time to reflect on the "why's" and "what-for's" of my crisis as it unfolded.

Personal growth comes in all shapes and sizes. It's not always simple and easy as planting a seed, watering it well and sitting back to watch it bloom into what you desired at the time. My crisis, although deeply painful, was an opportunity for me to grow and continue to move forward. No looking back, I said! As hard as this bitter pill was to swallow, the tools I've been given helped me understand that a "tight spot" gives us the opportunity to mature. This realization of the matter made the sting of un-reconciliation with my mother and her passing more endurable. I can't change what will never be, but I am determined to learn from it and to not allow the same outcome of me and my mother to happen with me and my children.

As I sat in the limousine, travelling to my mother's internment, I looked at my four grown children and in their tear laden eyes of sadness yet with strength, assertiveness and determination -all at the same time, they would never ever sit where I was sitting at the moment; not knowing if their beloved mother had ever loved them or the person she had become. I assured my children life was too precious to waste valuable energy in hurt feelings, thoughts or words. One day I too will pass on and in that instant they will always know how very proud I am of them and how I love them dearly. As we embraced this moment in time, the monster that had possessed my mother died along with her – never to be given a breath of life again.

I didn't have the answers before as to why my relationship with my mother was the way it was and I didn't understand the "why's" and the lesson that was attached to my unanswered questions. But, one day, as the healing of my wounds will take place, in and with time, the "aha moment" will scream to me the answers I have spent a lifetime seeking and in that split second, without a doubt, I will celebrate this situation. I thus decided, then and there, to let go and continue on my journey; no regrets, blame, guilt, or self-admonishment. My circumstance unfolded exactly as it was meant to and everything happens for a reason. I accept the fact that she did the best she could and her spirit will always be with me. I am proud to be her daughter and I know because she was who she was- unknowingly she had helped me to be the person I am today. All in all, I've reconciled in my soul "this too shall pass" Now, onto the life I was designed live.

It's not the smooth passages on our journey that reveals the light bulbs of new and precious understandings. It is the strenuous uphill battles, twist and turns, falling off the mountains of challenges, or stumbling through deep puddles of reasoning that all benefit us with the valuable knowledge we need to learn to grow into our potential. I understand and embrace now, that a crisis is not a crutch or a stumbling block meant to cripple me in my tracks. It can be a gift, a blessing in a masquerade, so well done that the most seasoned of actors might pass the role by instead of embracing and acting out its scene. These gifts bring about resolutions, promises a greater comfort to us, and we end up looking upon them as prized possessions – willing to be shared so others can benefit.

With reflection of this past month, I see now that without this crisis, I would not have been able to climb higher in the ladder of life. The death of my mother, without closure or resolution of conflict, was an important rung on that ladder. I also had to step up to the plate – learn what I needed to learn or "crash and burn". Stepping out of my comfort zone, I refused to stagnate and stop growing. I refocused my energies into viewing this situation in the positive.

As I finish my first half-century on this planet, I believe I have just experienced a true mid-life crisis. This experience is a result of sensing the passing of one's own youth and the imminence of their old age," but a true crisis – one that I can look at and confidently call a blessing.

I have endured many late nights in the lessons library researching my life's path with all its twists and turns. I am now a graduate and it is time to rejoice in the blessings of it. I must admit, this has been a tough journey, but I did my best to rectify the situation to no avail of my own and now I must stand back and admire this newly attained diploma of "hard knocks" and smile. At this time, I say out with the thought of – "Crisis" and in with the thought – "Blessings."

Life can be over so quickly without any notice at all. Just when we get on the right tract, life can end just as quickly, and we either come out a little wobbly or we can succumb to the injuries. I chose to pick myself up, brush the dirt from my knees and move forward. I no longer become too embroiled in attaching my self-worth to others (my mother in particular) and situations.

I realize death brings our mortality to the surface. I plan to slow down and live more. I have accumulated all the items I need right now and I am content. I eagerly embrace my spirituality and stop to smell the roses more often than in the past. Each rose is pretty anytime of year.

In the past, I spent so much time and energy focusing on the expectation of reconciling with my mother, when the goal didn't materialize, I was devastated. It was only until I came to the understanding that I am to set my goals, but I must release all expectations of how I think I am going to attain them. On my journey, I realize I must keep an open-mind and get out of the way as life unfolds itself.

My situation has also strengthened my resolve to continue to embrace life with no regret or guilt – challenges, problems or transitions which are naturally avoided. But, if I were to be really honest, life would be incredibly boring without them. Hurdling tests in life causes us to grow and blossom, achieve dreams and go for the gold.

Stagnation has no room in my life. I understand now that knowing every day would be the same as the next, would take the motivation from our sails and our dreams probably would not come to fruition. However, I must admit, with this comprehension, fear wants to rear its ugly head and keep me steadfast in the familiarity. But, I will practice courage and roar back with my lion's heart to become a great member of the fearless. We all have our fears. Doing something I am afraid to do help me grow. I know –going forward, I am going to defy the odds; one step at a time.

Perhaps, you too, have dreamed your whole life for something and it hasn't appeared yet- don't stop now, because you are just getting started with attaining all that you desire. You deserve it, live and celebrate it too.

Now, I finally got my fight back. I am taking this chance to reach out to my dad and family, and slowly build bridges; step by step. Bridges may be broken, but they have not washed away completely so with time and effort they can be restructured and become stronger than ever. I just have to have faith and believe. I am celebrating the restful period in my life and storing up strength and energy, for I realize that I have more tests ahead of me in my journey. I know now I'm enormously prepared.

> *"Every Stage of an experience has its roots in the past and leans towards the future. I'll trust whatever I encounter today, I believe I've been prepared for and will benefit from." – Karen Casey & Martha Vanceburg, Hazelden - Meditations*

4 Tips to Get Your Fight Back – From Crisis to Blessing

Open Your Eyes To The Lesson. A challenging transition can blind you to the "Aha" moment at hand. Any challenge masks the lessons that are before us. We may not understand the "why" and the lesson that is attached. But with time the lesson screams to us to listen and take notes. Every challenge is a chance to learn, grow, and move forward.

Savor Your Blessings. A crisis is not a crutch or stumbling block meant to ripple you in your tracks. A crisis is a blessing in masquerade. These blessings are gifts that bring about resolutions that promise greater comfort.

Keep Walking Forward. Comfort Zone can be crippling. Refuse to stay comfortable and in the familiar, even if it appears easier. Refocus your energies and view every situation in the positive and put one foot in front of the other and grow - blossom to your fullest potential. Step over the thresh-hold of your zone and walk proudly in the direction you are meant to walk.

Let Go – Release Expectations! Set your goals, but release all expectations of how you think you will attain them. So, keep an open mind and go with the flow – get out of the way. Life might very well have something better in store for you.

Your Unique Imprint
By Lezlyn Parker

Women are amazing. We work, parent, volunteer, try to maintain relationships...multi-taskers of extraordinary skill, right? Yes, until we wake up one morning and realize that we are, simply put, exhausted. In that moment, the idea of chugging through another day is more than we can bear. And you know the best kept secret about this exhaustion? It's happening to women all around us. Just the other day, I had a call from a woman who was at her end point and was looking for coaching. She and her husband were recent empty nesters, but an emotional gulf was growing between them. Her adult children took advantage of her because she struggled to set boundaries with them. And her career had stalled, leaving her in a different place than she had envisioned for this season of her life. She was exhausted and yearning for a different life that included healthier relationships with her family and a fresh approach toward her career.

Oh how my heart ached for this dear woman. I remember so well the times when I felt the weariness of life overtake me too. I lost my fight...that urge to bounce back when life walloped me one too many times.

Beaten Up By Life

For many of us, learning that we need to cultivate a "fighter" mentality is a lesson we learn early. My first memory of losing my fight goes back to my high school days. I will never forget when my math teacher asked me to go to the board and solve a problem. Why do teachers do this? I was terrified. I didn't understand the equation, but when I hesitantly told the teacher this, she blurted out, "What do you mean you don't know how to do it? It's not that hard!" Ugh. I reluctantly walked up to the board and scribbled something, hoping for the best. "Go sit down!" the teacher bellowed. My classmates snickered as I walked back to my seat, and I was upset for days. I'll give this teacher the benefit of the doubt about intending to humiliate me, but how could she be so insensitive? My confidence was shaken for years by this moment in high school math.

Thankfully, college taught me a different lesson. One of my required courses was Public Speaking. I prayed, "No, Lord. Please don't do this to me. I just can't stand in front people and speak to them." Fear coursed through me that my professor would embarrass me like my high school teacher had done. What a different experience this turned out to be. When I wanted to quit, he would encourage and affirm me. I stayed the course -- no pun intended – and facing my fear of failure helped me begin to get my fight back. Years later, I would speak nationally at conferences with my husband, and I credit my experience in *Public Speaking* in my ability to do this. Ladies, you can begin to get your fight back by courageously facing your fear of failure. Take a moment to think about what your fears might be and, more importantly, what you might accomplish if you faced them.

Another area ripe for practicing our "fight" is in choosing how we react to expectations other people hold for us. I remember my conference speaking work with my husband? At one of these events, a professional speaker/trainer who heard me speak invited me to lunch. While we ate, she said, "You're a good speaker. You capture the audience and they enjoy listening to you. But I have to tell you the negative side as well. You don't make eye contact and you try to win them by your smile. Just read from a script and you'll be okay." Wow, I could scarcely catch my breath! I just wasn't prepared for this feedback because this isn't what I was hearing from people in the audience. They expressed appreciation for my transparency and vulnerability. I had to make a choice conform to this professional's expectations of my speaking or hold true to what had worked for me. Rather than read from a script, I chose to "tear up the script" and be who I was. Too often as women, we find ourselves giving in to the expectations others have for us. Stand firm. Find your voice – your "you-uniqueness". You were not born to follow a script or to merely fit in. You were born to leave an imprint.

If fighting expectation is hard, standing firm in the comparison game is even harder. She has a nicer house, bigger car, thinner thighs! Why do we do this to ourselves as women? We are so quick to go negative, putting down our looks, our accomplishments, our spouse, our children. For me, it's a "weighty" issue that has dogged me for years. I used to secretly wish I could look like a model or trade places with one of my girlfriends that had no weight issues. There are still days I can look in the mirror and say to myself, "You look so fat! Who could ever want you?" STOP the madness! If you identify with this, it's time to get your fight back by refusing to play the comparison game. It's not a fun game and there are no winners. Get your fight back by doing the most with what you've been given by God as it relates to your body, your marriage, your kids, your abilities. Remember, God's beauty contest is measured by your inner qualities and what you do with them. Each of us is uniquely crafted by Him to be who we are fight on!

Lacing Up the Boxing Gloves

Ladies, here are some other life-enhancing principles that have made an impact in my life. Remember, no matter what has happened in your life, it is never too late to get your fight back. You can be resilient and bounce back!

Here are a few suggestions to follow:

- **Accept responsibility for our life.** It is time to grow up. Children blame others when things don't go their way, but

GROWN-UP men and women accept full responsibility for their behavior. I had to stop blaming people for why things didn't work out for me. I had to stop acting like a victim and begin acting like a victor. One of my husband's favorite sayings is, "It takes a healthy me to build a strong we." We become healthy as we accept responsibility for our lives.

• **Surround yourself with spiritually and emotionally healthy women.** When I realized that I wanted a different life path, I had to change the group of women that I spent time with. My friends weren't bad people, but we did not share the same values and were not heading in the same direction. I needed to be with women who were wise in how they fought back from the bruises of life. I now have seasonally mature women who mentor and coach me in how to make choices that allow my life to flourish.

• **Invest in reading and journaling.** I heard someone say, "Every great leader is a reader." For me, books are a type of personal life coaching. I may never meet the authors, but they serve as my coaches through their insights and information. Journaling helps me to clarify my thoughts. Through journaling I self-assess by asking questions such as: What am I learning? What can this situation teach me about God, people, and me?

Life is hard. If you find yourself running on empty, don't worry. You are among a large group of women that are facing the same struggle. Take a breath and begin to get your fight back.

With some time, attention and tenderness, you can take your life from good to great!

4 Tips to Get Your Fight Back – Be Yourself

Face Your Fear Of Failure. Failure is excellent in training. What would you do or say if you weren't afraid?

Dare Not To Compare. Embrace your gifts and abilities.

Find Your Voice. Celebrate your "you-uniqueness" and leave an imprint wherever you go.

Accept Responsibility For Your Life. A great life doesn't happen automatically, it is built intentionally. Take ownership of your life.

Forget Not From Where You Came

by Rosalind Y. Tompkins

I was sitting in the visiting room of a State Correctional Facility in Georgia, after having just performed a bitter sweet wedding ceremony for one of my members, a dear sister filled with wide eyed optimism and faith, believing for a miracle saying how can you not get caught up in the intoxication of fresh love and hope even in the midst of barbed wired fences, cement walls and prison doors? As I sat there in the midst of the conversation that had quickly turned to talk of alcohol and partying lifestyles, the mother of the groom said to her children, "Please remember that we have a Pastor among us." I, without hesitation, opened my mouth to join in for the first time with the words, "don't worry I've been there." There was a hush that went over the room as all eyes turned to me as I sat there in my Kay Barry Original black and red robe with a red cross sashayed across my right shoulder and I said, "Yeah, I talk about it in my first book, *"As Long As There Is Breath In Your Body, There Is Hope"* how I went through the my addition of **crack-cocaine,** and now

I am over twenty years -- free and clean." Eventually the conversation began again all around me but the mother of the groom leaned in her seat closer to me and began to share her story and how she struggled with addiction. At one point she said, "but since it has been so long for you, you are probably out of touch." I looked at her with eyes filled with compassion, smiled, shook my head and said, "I will never forget where I came from!"

It all began when I was twelve years old. I was a straight - A- student in school. I was very bright, but very mischievous or "bad" as my momma called it. I grew up living in the household with my mother, step father, my brother who is three years older than I. My sister, who had already left for college, was nine years older than I too.

One evening when I came home from school my brother asked me to come into the back yard to play basketball with him. We had a makeshift rim nailed to a tree where we would practice making shots. I said okay, because my mother had not made it home from work and I wasn't doing anything but looking at television. When I got outside my brother pulled out a joint, lit it and inhaled. He breathed out this oddly sweet smelling smoke that filled the backyard. At first I thought it was a cigarette which wasn't unusual, because we had smoked before. However, the smell was different and the cigarette looked different too. He asked if I wanted to try some "weed." I had been taught about drugs in school and I knew that they were bad for you so at I said, "No". I changed my mind when I realized he didn't really want to play basketball. So, I said "okay, let me try it", which he did, and the rest as they say is history.

I started to smoke marijuana regularly with my brother and cousins who were introduced to drugs by my brother as well. This was the other mixture, because my brother had his learner's permit to drive, we would go riding and smoke "reefer" just about every weekend. Needless to say, this became a habit and all we did was get high. My brother went on to use harder drugs as he graduated from high school and made his way to college. One might wonder did my mother know that we were using drugs, well the answer is no. She did not know and as a matter of fact she thought we were all literally crazy especially me. All during high school I was sequestered in my room 24/7 except for when I went to school and out to parties. My mother and I didn't talk at all and I stayed out later than I should had been able to, then I would sneak into the house. The summer after I graduated high school and was accepted into Florida State University, she sent me to stay with my sister and her husband in Miami, because I was out-of-control.

The greatest thing which happened to me at that time was an event that I will never forget as long as I live. My sister and her husband had come to pick me up and we were headed from Pensacola to Miami. They decided to stop and spend the night in

Tallahassee to visit his brother who was attending college there. Also, let me point out that my sister had accepted Jesus Christ as her Lord and Savior a few years earlier. Now don't get me wrong, we were raised as Christians and we attended Bethel A.M.E. church regularly as we were growing up. However, it was mostly a religious family ritual more than anything else. I never knew that there was more to it and that you could have a personal relationship with the God that I heard about Sunday after Sunday. That night in Tallahassee, Florida I accepted Jesus into my heart for the first time. My birth in the Kingdom wasn't your normal rebirthing experience. I was sitting in the living room reading an Essence Magazine and my sister came in and asked me if I ever read the Bible. I said, "No, not really" then she picked up the Bible and shared with me the plan of salvation. I listened closely as she asked me if I would like to be "saved" and accept the Lord into my heart. Several things flashed through my mind with the dominating thought being, "I am going to be stuck with them all summer long, so I better go ahead and do this to get it over with so they can leave me alone." With that in mind, I bowed down on my knees and bowed my head and began to pray with her and repeat these words, "Father God I acknowledge that I am a sinner, please forgive me for all of my sins and Jesus, come into my heart and be my Lord and Savior. I thank you for dying on the cross for me and I confess with my mouth and believe in my heart that you are Lord." After saying that prayer, even though I wasn't sincere about it at first, something changed in me and it was this very event that saved me from eternal hell both on earth and in eternity. This event turned the tide on the devil's ultimate plan for my life although it would be several years before I was actually set Free.

We made it to Miami and I started attending church regularly with my sister. The only problem was that my brother also lived in Miami with his soon to be wife; therefore, I could go over to his house and smoke marijuana whenever I could. The twist is - this is my same brother, who I had previously got high with back home, he was now in Florida. This change of event allowed there to be an open door to keep the drugs in my life. As a matter of fact, I tried powder cocaine for the first time that summer before heading to college. So, I started college, back-sliding, with an addiction to marijuana, and a habit of snorting cocaine when I could afford it. Once there, I quickly found others who also used drugs. One summer when I was only nineteen years old I was using hallucinogenic mushroom tea and I had a particularly bad trip that led me to psychiatric hospitals on four different occasions. By the Grace of God, I was healed and restored and I eventually went back to college only to begin hanging out in a place called Frenchtown which was a hot spot for drugs. It was there that I met someone who eventually introduced me to crack-cocaine.

Crack-cocaine possessed me and caressed me and eventually became me and I became it. I say that because while using the drug, I disappeared into a "ghost". The real Rosalind ceased to exist and what was left was a hallow shell in a zombie like state, programmed to smoke crack. For the first time in my addiction, I realized that I definitely had a problem. I wanted to stop using and I eventually did when I got pregnant and had a still born baby girl six months into my pregnancy. Finally I asked the question, "Why, God?" I re-opened the dialogue that I had shut down with my Creator. I became humble to the point of surrender when I ended up getting my heart broken and found myself pregnant again. "This time will be different", I told myself and I finally stopped using all drugs for the first time in twelve years! When my baby girl, Janar came along everything changed. I found a small store front Word of Faith, Charismatic, Non-Denominational church and begin attending when she was but an infant. I never looked back. In 1991 I started the non-profit organization, Mothers In Crisis, Inc. to help women overcome drug and alcohol addiction. I was ordained as a minister of the Gospel and I founded Turning Point International church in 1998 where I currently serve as senior pastor. Over the past two decades we have helped thousands of families to overcome addictions.

Never Forget Where You Came From

I learned many lessons going through the world of substance abuse; mine specifically, crack-cocaine which I also outline in my first book "As Long As There Is Breath In Your Body, There Is Hope." I call them the eight pearls of wisdom: The Power of Love, The Power of Prayer, The Power of Resilience, The Power of Hope, The Power of Unity, The Power of Suffering and Humility, The Power of Passion, and The Power of Respect. These principles have shaped my life and helped me to walk a drug-free overcoming life for over twenty years and counting.

At this stage of my life, however, I must add to the list above -sustainability. The reason that this is important is, because I have seen too many women who have been clean and sober for years, sometimes, ten or more, go back to a life of drugs and alcohol. It is a habit that is very hard to break once you go back after several years of recovery or "freedom". I know that relapse is often a part of the recovery process, but it doesn't have to be. Especially after you make it through the first stages of recovery which usually last anywhere from two-five years. I have found that the reasons people go back to drug and alcohol addiction varies greatly, but there are guiding principles that will keep you if you want to be kept and remain free from its ugly, snaring grip.

"Never Forgetting Where You Came From" is a major principle that will help one to navigate through life drug and alcohol free. This principle has served me well to keep making the right decisions day by day, week by week, month by month, and year by year. While I never subscribed to the NA or AA Model of confessing that I was an addict after I got into recovery, I do understand the concept. It helps one to remember that *recovery is a life-long process and if you put the chemicals back into your body, the addiction will resurface. Many people do what it takes to get clean, but refuse to do what it takes to stay clean.* What I have found is that the method that got you clean is what you will need to hold onto for dear life -all of your life in order to maintain your sobriety. For me, it was my relationship with Jesus. When I reactivated and reconnected my life and love with my Savior, He made me whole. I surrendered my will to His will. Now if I decided that I no longer needed God, I know it would only be a matter of time before I went back to using drugs.

Many times addicts let go of God, people and the things that helped them to get and stay clean. The deception is, they forget from whence they come. They sometimes, also, coupled with lies from the devil and others they use to keep company with while smoking drugs, maybe even their inner self, begin to get a false impression; they think because they're now living productive lives, i.e., maybe they have good jobs with steady streams of income, are in good relationships, have material possessions, etcetera., they are "cured" and no longer have to remember that they were once addicted to drugs. This can really work against you because addiction is cunning and very powerful. I have seen so many people lulled into a false sense of security thinking they can drink alcohol like regular people who are not addicts or alcoholics. They began by drinking a glass of wine or a beer and before long it escalate and they become full blown alcoholics or they go back to their drug of choice. This also happens at an alarming rate with prescription drugs. Doctors oftentimes prescribe powerful narcotics to recovering addicts, because they have genuine need of pain medication. The only problem is that with continued use your brain will pick it up as another "fix" and before long you can become addicted to pain pills. I had surgery several years ago and during and after the operation, I was given narcotics- was prescribed powerful pain killers to take home. Because I "never forgot where I came from", I monitored my usage of the prescription drugs. While I was using the prescription pain killers I had crack dreams like I hadn't experienced in years, because to my brain a drug is a drug. As soon as I started feeling better I stopped using them and used over the counter pain medication instead.

Shame and guilt are major reasons that people forget where they came from. I've seen pastors and speakers who have testimonies of deliverance refuse to share, because they do not want people to know where they have been. What I have found is that in order for you to truly know me you need to know where I've been. While my past doesn't define me, it helps to refine me for my journey. I have shared my testimony before the Senate for the State of Florida, in the Governor's Mansion and on street corners. I like to say, "I will tell it from the white house to the outhouse, it doesn't matter!" The reason why, is because I keep what I have by giving it away to someone else. At the time that I shared with the Senate, Governor Jeb Bush and his wife were there and they were experiencing addiction first hand with their daughter, Noel, who was all over the news for getting arrested for falsifying prescriptions for pain killers. My testimony gave them hope at a time that they really needed it.

4 Tips to Get Your Fight Back – From Addiction

Keep Your Story Fresh, New, and Ever Before You. It may not be drug addiction, but each of us has a story to tell. You can keep yours fresh by finding appropriate groups to share with that will benefit from what you have learned. Many youth organizations need mentors who have actually experienced some of the obstacles that they are facing. You can volunteer your time and help others to navigate through life by learning from your failures and successes.

Maintain a Campaign of Self-Awareness. As you share with others it becomes increasingly important to be authentic. The last thing you want to do is to attempt to teach others what you can't do. You must be congruent and in touch with YOU- spirit, soul, and body. This means taking care of your inner and outer world.

Never Stop Learning Knowledge, Information, and Revelation. Always remain a student in life who is teachable, trainable, and coachable. This will insure that you never stop growing. It's good to be informed with wisdom, understanding, and knowledge but please don't stop there, you also need revelation so that you will know how to apply what you have learned.

Never Forget Where You Came From. As the saying goes, "Those that forget the past are doomed to repeat it." While we definitely should not live in the past, we should never forget where we have come from. We should remember the past on a feeling level and remember what it really felt like to go through some of the things that you went through. This helps you to genuinely relate to others who are going through the same things.

No Limits
by Sandra J. Bradley

I knew the day would come when I would have an opportunity to tell my story. So allow me to begin: My name is Sandra J. Bradley. I was born in New York City. From my mother, I am an only child. I grew up in the city and my mom worked hard to take care of me. I went to Catholic school, and enjoyed some things that my other friends did not have. One would say that from the outside my life looked wonderful. If you came in, you would have thought differently.

I am an over comer of incest and child molestation, from the age of six until I turned sixteen. My mom worked long hours and I use to go to "Grandma's" house. Grandma's husband would take me with him to church where he was the custodian. It was there he would molest me (in the baptismal pool). This is my moment of having the fight knocked out of me. I began to hate God and all that God stood for.

Also, from age nine till sixteen I was abused (by "Grandmother's" grandson and my biological Father). Throughout my life I had many ups and downs, twist and turns.

The connecting dots were the sexual abuse I had experienced in my early childhood into my teenage years.

On my journey, I joined the United States Navy, got married (to a man like my father), had a son, and attempted to live a good life. My children were my "saving grace" in many ways. Ernest (28) and Jasmine (24) helped me to keep my head above the water in many aspects. I taught my children to pray; however, God and I didn't have a relationship and no one could talk to me about God in my home.

My challenges came in the form of self hatred, and suicide. Suicide was like a blanket and I truly believed that 'it" loved me. I would wrap myself in the thought of leaving here and at times it would soothe the pain I was experiencing. I tried to kill myself six times, with the last time attempting to take my life and my children with me. However, there would soon come —my moment, a freedom I had never known nor experienced before.

One day my father passed. My sister and my husband knew my story. His death was another one of my "saving graces." Upon his death, at the funeral home, I was able to take his cold hand in mine and release all my agony, sorrow, and pain which had been bottled in me for many years. As I cried at the funeral, people may have assumed it was for my dad: it wasn't. The tears were for the little girl in me.

At some point, by God's grace, I accepted Jesus Christ and my Lord and Savior, but I did not believe that God loved me. I did not think highly of myself. The words that I had been told as a child haunted me. "You are so black no one can see you", "You're damaged goods. No one is going to want you." I had not learned how to love myself. My healing was a slow process. I look at myself now and wonder how I could have possibly survived. I stayed alive, overcame because of the Love of God.

I remember my pastor preaching one Sunday about the people that God places in our lives at a specific time. It was then that I believed God really did love me! I closed my eyes and looked at the women of God whom the Lord placed in my life and thought to myself how awesome He is!! I saw the faces of various individuals who God had strategically place in my life on my journey to discovering who I really was and who I would ultimately become. For instance, first the young lady that helped me as a teenager, I can still remember her laughter. Second, Ms- so and so, she looked out for me while being in the military at the age of sixteen. Thirdly, the lady who wipes my tears, because my husband had physically abused me and —oh how she encouraged me and the list goes on and on.

Now, I've gotten my fight back and you can too. At this point in time- in my life, I have tears of forgiveness, release and thankfulness. I realized the magnitude of how God loved me so much that He sent precious angles along the way -people to love on me and to encourage me on my journey called life. **I AM A SURVIVOR, and a THRIVER, WITH NO LIMITS!**

4 Tips to Get Your Fight Back - After Mistrust

First, you must fall in love with God, and then love yourself.

Even when you turn away from God, He will place people in your path to love on you, nurture you and help you.

There is a lesson in the bad experiences OF LIFE. We have to be able to look at the THEM and see something good in it. Our experiences help us improve our way of thinking; it opens our minds to new horizons and teaches us unforgettable lessons along the way.

Life is a win, win journey if we let it. You learn from *winning*, but you can learn even more from losing sometimes.

Define Your
Relationships

Pain ~ The Propelling Agent

by Mary Davisson

I 'm a mother, a published author, a friend, an aunt, feature writer for two magazines, an editor, divorcee, an entrepreneur, senior manager, ordained minister, preacher, teacher, speaker, life coach, business advisor, image consultant and I have the bomb "diggidy" friends and a few enemies too. Life just couldn't get any better. However, there was a period of time when I suffered a major health challenge, like David, I had to really encourage myself in the Lord. With all of the good things that I am doing and have done, I too, have had my share of having to -*Get my fight back.*

Have you ever been betrayed? A place you thought was a safe place to be yourself turned out to be a nightmare? Did you know Jesus was betrayed too? My story begins here; how to *"Get Your Fight Back"* -after an atrocious betrayal.

In my situation, I began to experience a lot of pain. I had trouble breathing, began to experience numbness in my legs, heart palpitations and often I felt like my breath was being cut off. I would go about my day and then suddenly out of nowhere the attack would come. It frequently happened at home, in my car, at work and on my way home from church, at the grocery store, wherever and whenever. Often, while driving, I had to pull on the side of the road because I could feel the "wind" being knocked out of me as I struggled to breathe. For the first time in my life, I was in a lot of pain and I didn't know what to do… For the first time in my life, I had no control over my body. This would go on and off for a year... When the attacks came, all I could do was moan like a wounded animal striving, fighting for its last breath. One day I decided to do research about my dilemma. I found out that my health challenge was all too common. It was GAD; severe panic disorders, attacks, heart palpitations. In my research, many people had experiences, symptoms of GAD after a major injury, physical, physiological or emotional trauma.

Did you know pain transcends ethnicity, social status, economic background, culture, gender, where you live, the kind of car you drive, the church you attend, education and religion. It means to cause mental or physical pain (verb); physical suffering or discomfort caused by illness or injury (noun). Pain casts its net universally with a worldwide language that speaks loud and clear to each of us. Everyone can relate to being injured at least once. However, did you know pain can either propel you further into your destiny or it can destroy you, here and now? I am a witness, pain, if we allow it, can be a propelling agent in our lives.

As I reflect upon that time, I equate my occurrence to Joseph in the bible, in Gen 37... However, before, I share my experience; I'd also like to share a dream that God gave me regarding the soon coming danger. In one of the darkest, trying times of my life, the dream helped me to know- during my season of testing, God was with me and I was not alone.

I was sitting at home chatting with some friends when suddenly an acrimonious animal came to the glass door. All we could see was its teeth! I signaled for someone to quickly close the door. However, before we blink an eye, it came running through the entrance, slid under the glass table, lunged at me and bit one of my hands. Instantly, fear gripped me! I could see the animal's teeth as it came out on the other side of my right hand. As I lifted my left hand to hit the creature, it bit my left hand in the same place. At that time, unexpectantly the dream switched to the next scene. I was in the next room and I noticed my hands were bandaged. As I went into the room one of the ladies – I will call her Cee- asked me to do something for her, but I couldn't because my hands were bandaged. At that point, another person- which I will call Linda- said in the dream- she can't do that -don't you see her hands are injured, don't you see the bandages? Cee- in the dream said, "no, she looks fine to me."

The dream troubled me for days. I kept asking God what the dreams meant and the heavens were silent!! I knew something horrible was about to happen. In dreams, your hands symbolize a means of support. The right hand represents power and strength, while the left hand signifies support, aid, and helper. As my world began to change, the dreams I had about a month earlier were now about to be played out in real life.

Some time ago, one of my co-labors in the ministry—I will refer to as Brey- I would soon realize this person sought more control in the ministry. We didn't always agree of course, but who does. For the most part, we did. Brey and I had developed a close relationship as friends and as workers in the vineyard. But, some people can't agree to disagree. They seek unknowingly and sometimes intentionally to be in control of you, the ministry God has given you, your career, in relationships, in your life, in the church, at work and with your children; it must be their way or no way. Brey couldn't support the direction that I felt God was leading me, so we mutually decided to part ways and that's ok. There was a time when Paul and Barnabas separated. ~ *Read Acts 15:36-41*~ Some people aren't meant to go to the next level with you and that's ok too.

However, it wouldn't be quite that simple because this person wasn't going to leave peaceably. As the situation began to intensify, I would soon found out there was another individual behind the scene who would become a key player in the game.

They begin to escalate the conflict instead of helping us to resolve it. I was startled when one day Brey admitted to disclosing their side of the private matter to others. Matter of fact, I saw the persons quite often and they acted like they didn't know anything. See, it's very easy for some of us to be pretentious, to wear a mask, believe lies, and distorted views about people because we don't like them anyway. We sometimes make quick judgments on the basis of what we hear and on what we think we know... Now, that is another story and perhaps another book.

Isn't it amazing, how we like to see, and quite as it's kept, we enjoy the annihilation of others; specifically Christians. We are so insecure with ourselves that we won't admit to the fact that we don't like others simply because we are secretly jealous and envious of them? They have something that we want or feel we are entitled to have. We like to hear mean, hateful, negative comments about people-whether it's true or not. Sometimes we even participate in the injury which is occurring in their life because we don't like them for whatever reason. Tell me, how do we sleep at night? The bible says the heart is desperately wicked! ~ *Jeremiah 17:9.* Although the heart is wicked, some of us aren't asking God to do anything about our evilness. We aren't ashamed of it; rather, we make excuses for staying that way, some take pride in it and gloat about it. Trust me, if you want to change, God will transform you. However, if you want to remain the same, He will allow you to stay that way; he will give you over to the thing that drives you; good or bad. Holla!

We don't preach or talk a lot about it today; nevertheless, it is a major problem in our communities, at work, in the world and in the church. We act like it isn't there; however, it is alive and well! We condemn people in our minds and we send them to the guillotine before we know the facts? My mother has always said "the only people that really know what happened in a situation are those involved and God." What's even sadder is for some of us, we don't care if it isn't true; we like to see others hurting because we don't like them! Their pain somehow makes some of us feel better about ourselves that's how **low our self-esteem is** -now that is a *chilling* thought.

This situation allowed me to see that our enemies will come together at times to plan our defeat, assist with our execution and act like they didn't do a thing. They will smile in your face while planning your demise behind your back. I call this the "kiss of Judas." Ok, you say, prove it. I think I will. Let's go to Mark 3:6, KJV, *"Then the Pharisees went forth and straightway took counsel with the Herodians against him, how they might destroy him."* Look at how these two enemies, yet mighty forces, got together long enough to crucify our Lord. It was a known fact they didn't like each, were opposing forces- if you will, yet each of them had a common so called "enemy," in Jesus and we can see what happened to him? Need I say more...?

Remember the story of Joseph in the bible? He was a teenage boy receiving dreams from God about his future in Genesis chapter 37. Take note of Genesis chapter 45, NIV, *Joseph finally reveals himself before his brothers and the bible says that he wept so loudly, that the Egyptians and the house of Pharaoh heard it…* Wow! Can you imagine what was going through their minds when they heard Joseph's pain? I bet they were saying, what was that? Was that Joseph? I believe that was Joseph's day of vindication and total healing for what his brothers had done to him. His dreams had finally come to past. The author of Genesis penned Joseph's pain for the entire world to see. It was real and everybody heard him weep loudly -even his betrayers- whom were his brothers! That's where I was at the moment. I understood then and I understand now Joseph's agony, injury initiated and inflicted by his siblings. Whether it's your biological family members, co-workers or your brothers and/or sisters in Christ, the hurt, is real! Like P. Bunny Wilson said, 'betrayal is-its own baby" and it has its own set of roots that can run deep if left unattended!

The pain wouldn't go on forever. God heard me and wherever you are in life, he hears and sees you too! There I was, whether I wanted it to be or not; life had thrust me into a time span of critical decision making. Will I embrace this occurrence and allow pain to be the propelling agent in my destiny or would I give permission for it to eliminate me from the race? As I embarked upon my journey of pain, I would soon hear God say, *"You will live and not die; saidt the Lord and you will declare the works of God!!" ~ Psalm 118:7.* That rhema word from God spoke life to my debilitated body and death had to flee. Instantly, I knew I was healed as I heard and continued to embrace those words. Eventually my healing took place in totality. Yes, God did execute justice in my situation and yes, this painful time would arrest me and propelled me into my next level in God, as a published author, mother, human being, minister and in my career.

Perhaps in your world too, on your job, in the church and in other high places there are people who feel they hold your life, destiny, and future in their hands; they try to break you, to manipulate the events of your life and some even think you can't make a move unless they ok it. Let me sound the alarm of a controlling spirit; better known as a jezebel spirit. Oh, by the way, a jezebel spirit can live in a man and a woman. Although in the book of Revelations, the bible depicts it in a woman name Jezebel, it can possess men too. And believe me; it currently operates in some of our churches, people and outside of the church as well. God never intended for us to be manipulated, controlled, dominated or to become a "copycat" of anyone else's ministry, gifts, talents, life nor did he mean for us to be held captive by others. I know what it's like to have a Judas at work, in ministry, as a neighbor and in the church. But remember,

Jesus had one too. The scripture says a servant isn't greater than his master. *~John 15:20.* If Jesus had one in his ministry and life, we will have them too. So, get up, *"Girl, Get your Fight Back."*

Let's go back to Joseph in the bible for a moment? Joseph had visions from God as a young teenager, but they didn't come to past until he was much older and look at all he went through before it ever manifested. Now, if he was alive today, we would have labeled him prideful, arrogant and a lunatic, false prophet; perhaps even a person who had even missed God. After all, the man was in prison! Can't you hear the people saying who does he think he is anyway, they say he raped the "Kings" wife and that's why he's in prison? We wouldn't care about that he was falsely accused. Can't you see the modern day headlines plastered everywhere? *MAN, DREAMER WITH THE COAT OF MANY COLORS GOES TO JAIL FOR RAPE....*

Now, let's take a look at David's life. He was anointed as king as a youngster and his vision didn't come to past until he was in his thirties. Well, he ended up in Saul's palace, but the man was envious and jealous of him. Have you ever had a boss who was jealous of you and tried everything they could to destroy you -every chance they got? Saul chased David for years to kill him and David ended up sleeping in the wilderness and in caves. How do you like that, the man of God- David- you know the one Samuel anointed to be King one day- was now **homeless** at the hands of Saul? Can you imagine what people, his family was saying about him? *MAN, ANOINTED AS THE NEXT KING IS NOW HOMELESS!!*

What about Abraham, a Prophet, he was told he would be the father of many nations, but the words spoken to him by God which I'm sure he shared with others on his journey didn't come to past until he was 100 plus years old? His body and Sarah's were dead and beyond child bearing years. Back in those days, if you couldn't have children, it was a disgrace. Can you imagine the humiliation, what they (family, friends, at work, in the synagogues and the community) were saying about her not being able to bear her husband a son after so many years? After all, additionally, back in those days, when women birthed sons for their husband was very notable. On a different note, can you imagine what people were saying about Abraham? I'm sure they labeled him as a false Prophet, a man who had missed God; in view of the fact, he was still childless. But, I don't want to leave you hanging; he and Sarah would go on to birth the child of promise- Isaac.

There are many other heroes in the bible who have similar testimonies, a promise from God. They too, would go through painful times, misunderstandings, mockery and even shame before their long awaited dreams would ultimately come to pass. We say to the Lord, God use me; nonetheless, we want to determine how he does it. We want to control the how, when, and the where. The pulpit isn't the only place God can and will use you. Joseph was a modern day "Administrator" with a degree in "foreign administration" and "international affairs and currency." God can use you to write books, songs, at work, in your family, in your business, in ministry, as a producer, and at home, but we must remain open to his direction. Do yourself a favor and quit trying to control your life and God! This means beloved, sometimes, we are going to be in hand-selected, hand-picked, very uncomfortable, God ordained, God allowed, even painful situations. Jesus, told Peter, up to this point you've gone wherever you wished, but there will come a time where it won't be so -speaking of the death and crucifixion of Peter; how he would die. Jesus went on to say to Peter, someone else will lead you to a place you don't want to go ~ *John 21:18* Isn't that just like us; we don't always want to go down the road which Jesus has destined us to go.

On my journey, I learned, we must reprogram our minds to trust God no matter what! The battle is ultimately won in our minds. Sometimes people will lie on us, someone close to us will die, children may stray from their Christian roots, divorce may occur after twenty two years of marriage, pink slips will come, a teenage daughter gets pregnant, a close partner and business associate betrays you. Or maybe you've waited for your mate and now you can't have children. What will you do? How will you respond? Who knows what the future holds for each of us? In our darkest of night and in painful times, I am a living witness God will never leave you nor forsake you. *~Hebrew 13:5*

There are also times when God allows others to see us being wronged, even our pain; nevertheless, there are epochs when he doesn't. I didn't always feel, I would like nor live to tell my story. However, I am alive and I am thriving in-spite of it all! The pain was real; yet the injuries we experience can at times serve as propelling agents in our destiny. So, wait on the Lord in your difficulty, because he will empower you to always win.

How did I get through it all? It was my quite times with the Lord, the word of God coupled with prayer. Being intentional about standing on his promises, I listened to praise and worship music, ignored and rejected the "naysayers." I knew and know vengeance belonged to God; therefore, I didn't seek to take matters into my own hands and rescue myself. But, I purposed to wait patiently for God to do what he said he would do. I also surrounded myself with "like faith" minded people during the storm too. This is where I've drew from then, and I continue to draw from this place even now. *"History, despite its wrenching pain, cannot be unlived, but if faced with courage, need not be lived again. ~Mayo Angelo.*

So, right now, I speak life to every wound, cut, emotional, scars, physical, verbal and psychological injury and I declare to you today, *"you shall live and not die, and declare the works of God."*

For such a time as this, we were born, so we would *delineate, illustrate, and demonstrate* the greatness of our God!

Without the pain of betrayals baby, I wouldn't had been able to stand in other areas of my life when I needed to be a light in dark places and for the Kingdom of God. Nor would I be co-writing this book or sharing my, -the testimony of ~*I shall live and not die, but declare the works of God*…..

Take it from me, when pain is processed as it should, it can be a *propelling agent* in your life; ultimately catapulting you into new dimensions, greater heights in God, with a 20/20 vision of your purpose.

4 Tips to Get Your Fight Back – Pain and Betrayal

Stop- Remember, the ultimate battle is won in your mind. So, remain steady, focus on the positive, and reject the loser mentality. Regardless of what you are going through, tell yourself God is the umpire of your soul and he is definitely the pilot in your life. You must be deliberate about trusting God in-spite of what's going on in the natural. The word says the "Just shall live by faith and without faith it's impossible to please God." He will rescue you in time!

Look- Remember, God wants us to have 20/20 vision. Look at all he has done for you in the past and what he has brought you through thus far. If you stand still, trust and believe, you will see him do it again. While on this journey called life; at work and in ministry always pray for wisdom and guidance as you face your hurling storms and tests. It's a known fact that sometimes your relationships will be tested. If they don't stand the trial, test -it's ok to move on.

Listen- Remember, God will never leave you nor forsake you in your darkest night. Although, you may feel like he has; rest assure, he is always there. Listen for God's voice of triumph and victory, not the whispers of the naysayers, "small minded" people and your accusers. Dream big, be big, execute big and remain big!

Wait- Remember, they that wait upon him (God) shall renew their strength. God's strength is really made perfect only when we wait; give in to him. As a matter of fact, his strength can really be seen in a huge way when we are weak, in our weaknesses. Secondly, don't wrestle with, try to manipulate life to get the upper hand in your situation and tests, rather let go, and let God; I guarantee, you will see his glory if you do. It's been demonstrated time and time again, God's will is for us to always win!

Forgive Or Not Forgive
by Courtney Artiste

We have decided that your services are no longer needed, were the words that I heard on August 7, 2008 from the other end of the phone. The call had come from the Director of Nurses of the nursing home where I had worked for two years as a practical nurse. And though I didn't know it at the time, those words that seemed to haunt me in my dreams were the very words that set into motion a lesson that would change my life forever. I was totally devastated.

To be honest, I really wasn't sure why the situation affected me the way it did, because I never really liked the job anyway nor the people I worked with, and on top of that, it had been a constant battle for me to keep my job. But, the pay was good so I stayed despite the signs that I shouldn't have. For the first time in my life, I had been fired and the rage was rekindled every time I had to write the word "terminated" on a job application. The real battle began the day they denied my unemployment. In that moment, I felt the fight was knocked out of me.

Up to this point in time, I had just been hurt, now I was angry. I wanted revenge. Just when I thought, I had gotten over the situation, I had round two being played out in my life. I become completely consumed with anger and bitterness. I could hardly think about it without my eyes welling up with tears, and it seemed that every time I closed my eyes, I could hear those words and see the faces of the three people who had maliciously caused me to lose my job. I remember lying awake at night wishing that something terrible would happen to them or their children. I literally hated them and I wanted them to hurt as bad as I thought they had hurt me.

One day a couple of months later, as I was sitting on the side of my bed trying to scrape up enough money to buy my son a $12 pair of football socks, I remember feeling as if the weight of the whole world was on my shoulders and the passionate anger and hatred towards my former bosses burned so deeply within me that I could hardly stand it anymore. I recall asking God why he had allowed this to happen to me. My children didn't deserve this. In that moment I heard the voice of God say "I need to use you, but your heart is not right. Yes, they lied on you and they undermined you; however, you must forgive them and let it go." I fell to the floor as I was overcome with emotion because it didn't seem fair to forgive them, I also knew I hadn't deserved what they had done to me, but more importantly I didn't know how to let go. What I did know was this, the burden of unforgiveness had become too much for me to bear, so I asked the Lord to show me how to forgive them. He answered my prayer.

Believe it or not, there is more to life than our human eyes can ever see or our minds would ever comprehend. This is important to know because, at all times in an unseen arena, there is a war going on for our souls, our productivity, our peace, and our wellbeing. There are snares, and roadblocks that have been set up with primary purpose to derail our destiny.

There are people and situations that the adversary (the devil) has strategically placed in our pathway to get us off track. *1 Peter 5:8 says that the adversary as a roaring lion walketh about seeking whom he may devour (KJV)*. Unforgiveness is one of those snares. It is often said that forgiveness is for the one who is offended rather than the offender because it is highly unlikely that the three women in my situation ever thought about me again. Yet, at nearly every waking moment I thought of them. Unforgiveness is like a slow growing cancer. It eats away at you until there's nothing left except the smoldering pieces of your broken emotions. It is a sin unto death. Unforgiveness will drain you of your livelihood. It will leave you broken and incomplete.

Knowing I should forgive and making the decision to forgive were entirely different. Forgiveness is not something that just happened because I decided I should. Even after I made the decision to forgive my offenders, I continued to struggle with the emotions of the hurt I had experienced. The fruits of unforgiveness were deeply rooted and I knew it. Until the process of cultivation took place, forgiveness did not happen. Cultivation means to bring all materials that rob you of your growth to the surface of your heart so that you can address them and replace them with the good things needed to walk in your destiny. God wants us to be fulfilled and live joyous and fruitful lives, but until our hearts are right towards Him and others, we will remain barren. The bible says, while we were yet sinners Christ paid the price for us. Forgiveness does not depend on who is wrong or right. In the book of Acts, as Stephen was being stoned to death, he asked the Lord to forgive his offenders. Even Jesus who hung on the cross as a perfect and blameless man asked God to forgive His accusers. Forgiveness is a process and it requires action, focus, tenacity, maturity, and determination. Forgiveness is a matter of the heart; it really is. How about you? Do you know of anyone you need to forgive and release in and from your psyche?

The act of forgiveness goes against our very nature. Emotions are natural reactions to injustices. However, it is not our place to judge the other person or persons involved. *Luke 6:37 says Judge not, and ye shall not be judged: condemn not, and ye shall not be condemned: forgive, and ye shall be forgiven. (KJV)* So, the key to forgiveness is learning to control your emotions and it all begins with a choice and a deliberate act of your will. The reality of my situation was I didn't feel the people who had hurt me deserved to be forgiven, yet I wanted to live a blessed and fruitful life. Knowing this, I knew, I could never have it unless my heart was right. This became the driving force for me to let go of my hurt and pain, and my motivation to persevere when I considered not allowing the agony of my situation to dictate my actions. In my life, I was deliberate and intentional in walking in forgiveness. Unforgiveness can never be justified, regardless of the severity of it. The Bible commands us on more than one occasion to forgive others as God has forgiven us. We must forgive by faith and out of obedience; this is what I had purposed in my mind, spirit and soul to do.

Did you know information starts with environmental stimuli that enter our sensory memory through sight, hearing, or touch? In turn, this information then leaves the sensory memory and enters the short term memory (the mind). Information that you do not attend to is lost. Simply put it is forgotten. Only by rehearsal can information pass from the short-term memory to the long term memory (the heart). So, it is with unforgiveness. The consistent rehearsal of the painful event enables it to leave your mind and enter your heart causing it to become hardened and eventually deep-seated bitterness and anger will set in. >>>>I learned how to truly forgive through a man of God who is now my mentor and spiritual father. God taught me to forgive by the principle of saturation. This principle involved sabotaging the thoughts of the injustices by saturating my mind with the simple consistent, confession "I choose to forgive just as God forgave me." Throughout the day and night, I would make my confession. I wrote it on index cards and sticky notes and placed them in various places throughout my home and on the dashboard of my car. I wrote the names of the three women on a piece of paper and three times a day, whether I felt like it or not, I would pray for them and their families. As I acted upon the advice given to me, I was rewarded, little by little; the pain and the hurt began to dissipate.

As I state before, at the time, it was hard for me to understand why the situation affected me the way that it did. Today, I understand God's ways aren't like ours. His way of doing things is unique and sometime foreign to us. I know now the whole ordeal was allowed by God, so by firsthand experience, I can teach others about the power of forgiveness.

A few months later, as I was walking into the football stadium, I saw the woman who had approved the decision to terminate my employment. It had been a while since I had even thought about the incident. My heart started racing as I walked towards her, embraced her, greeted her and gave her a hug, then I walked away. It was an amazing feeling and although the memory of the situation was vivid, the sting of the unforgiveness had been removed- I was free! My life has never been the same after that moment. I have a peace beyond words. That was the day; I knew I had gotten my fight back.

If you are allowing your past to keep you from your future; my story can be your story. *Jeremiah 29:11 says that He knows the plans He has for you, plans to prosper you, and not to harm you, plans to give you hope and a future.* God knows your beginning to your end. He knew you before you entered your mother's womb. He knows every struggle, every tear cried, and every mistake you've made. He loves you with a love that your natural thinking and human imperfections cannot begin to comprehend and it gives Him great pleasure to see you flourish and live life full circle. Make a decision today to move from under the weight of unforgiveness and "step into your greatness." Surrender your will to his and rest in his amazing miracle working love, while allowing him to saturate you with the power of forgiveness.

4 Tips to Get Your Fight Back - Forgiveness

There is power in forgiveness. So, make a choice today to forgive. When you do, you will see God vindicate you in full.

Forgiveness does not depend on who is wrong or right. It really doesn't matter anyway because what's done is done.

Unforgiveness is never justifiable regardless of the severity of the offense. So, be intentional about executing forgiveness in your life regardless of whose fought it is.

You can never possess God's best or walk in all that He has for you by harboring unforgiveness. So, carve out the steps in your life that will take you down the road to forgiveness, success and full victory.

Tragedy To Triumph
by Denise Wilkins

A mother's triumphant return from the sudden death of her son

I t was approximately 8:00 am on Sunday morning, February 28, 2010, when I received a call that no committed Christian mother ever expects to receive. The voice on the other side of the phone says, "I am the weekend doctor at Central State Mental Hospital's Forensic Unit, and I am calling to inform you that this morning your son Justin was found dead in his bed." All I remember is dropping the phone, falling to the floor, making it to the bed in my room; I was rolling and screaming at the top of my lungs, "My baby! My baby! No not my baby!" Everything seemed surreal; I had always believed that Justin would live through this huge trial and come out with a great testimony. What do I do now, I said? Here in lays the fight being knocked out of me. I remember making one call to my sister, then time stood still for me and it seemed in an instance the house was filled with people. My numb body sat staring out into space as I lived what appeared to be a horrible nightmare.

(Twenty years earlier)

I'm a single mother, with three beautiful children. Regretfully, I did not raise my oldest son. At seven, he went to live with his father in Texas, we have sense been reunited. I entered full time ministry when my youngest children were three and seven. Believe it or not, my "sold out" lifestyle came as a shock to family and friends.

I had come to a point in my life, where I thought I could not continue. I accepted the fact that I was a total failure at life and wanted to stop trying to make something better that obviously was not getting better, so, I thought.

While sitting, crying hysterically, convinced that suicide was my only option, I had a vision. I saw myself standing on a stage with a microphone speaking to a group of people. I cried in amazement, as I belted out with fear and in tremble -I can't do that! Then, I heard an audible voice say to me, "there are no failures in God." This took place in 1991 and it would be five years later the vision I had originally experienced would actually manifest. From that day in time, to now- at the age of 34, his words to me were was simply, *GO YE! Go ye into the highways and the hedges and compel them to come in that my house may be filled. {Luke 14:23).*

For me, going back meant suicide, so despite the warfare, I learned to take authority in and over my life, and keep pressing forward to the prize in Christ Jesus *(Philippians 3:14).* My

58

commitment was established on this creed: A relationship with God; walking with God, knowing God, understanding God, the perfect will of God, the anointing of God will COST me something. The qualifying question; am I willing to pay the cost? My answer has always been yes!

Coming from a Catholic background, I was not quite prepared for an open vision and a call from God. In the past, I had never taken my faith seriously enough to believe that GOD was real. What I experienced at my desk, was so extreme, it triggered a greater awakening in me. I made a covenant with God that if he took my life and made it a success, I would follow him wherever He leads. From that moment on, I began my "sold out" life in Christ.

When God said, "meditate on His word day and night", I obeyed, no questions asked. I was immediately sensitive to the knowledge of a spiritual world, with an awareness of spiritual wickedness in high places *(Ephesians 6:12)*. When I started applying the word of God to my life and received the baptism of the Holy Spirit, I was birthed into the ministry of intercession with fasting and praying; it was then that the warfare in my life intensified.

Before joining a Church, I had spent quite some time studying the word of God and believe in the Holy Spirit being our guide *(John 16:13)*. As I embarked upon my new church experience, I was suddenly thrust into the Charismatic movement; whereby, its focus seemed to carry the implication that in order to be a spiritual giant you had to ask for, exemplify and obtain material wealth, prosperity. They taught us that your possessions was linked to spiritual maturity and security, and as a result, many lived under condemnation, that something was wrong with their faith because they had not obtained an enormous amount of material assets.

For Jesus' true followers, the Cross is not a piece of jewelry or even a symbol; it is a lifestyle, it is a heart that chooses to follow Christ and this means sometimes you will encounter sufferings. In order to do that, we must surrender ourselves and be willing to lay down our lives. We must have a fearless loyalty to God, no matter the cost, a total "buy-in" to the life, character, and way of Jesus. *I would soon find this out by way of personal experience.*

I use to host fun bible studies in my home for the youth, choreographed dances and street evangelism, coordinated evangelistic street meetings where we reached out in and to the community. For two years, at some point, I was asked to coordinate and oversee the "teen zone" of the "Convoy of Hope" mission which fed over 7000 families in the Metropolitan area.

Eventually, God allowed me to birth "The Christian Outreach Recreational Facility of the Artist" It's a center outside of the Church that teens can call their own; a place where they feel safe to develop a "teen culture." It is centered on values that will assist them as they navigate through the muddy waters of a liberal society.

After my children became teenagers, I went back to work. Strategically, God had blessed me to have jobs that were ministry-focused. One job in particular was a FEMA Funded program run by the Mental Health Department. My purpose was to evaluate the "state of the minds" of the youth and adults after the 9/11 attack on the Pentagon. After four years, the job with the City abolished and under the inspiration of the Holy Spirit, I wrote, directed and produced the stage play "Black Lights Shining in the Darkness".. God used this play to reach the youth, as many of them ran up to the altar of God to receive salvation. In all that I did for the Lord, my children were right by my side.

For seventeen years I worked in the ministry with huge success, just as God had promised. However, as an outsider looking one would think this woman of God has got it all together. But, behind the scenes, what they did not know was that on many occasions I had fought for my children's life; a struggle that only my close friends and family would know personally. My ministry was going great, but my natural life was literally falling apart all around me. It was a daily affair to care for my family. I felt like I was constantly under fire. People close to me didn't know how I was surviving.

I am not a perfect person, because when I came to Christ, I chose the Lord over my relationship with my children's father. His anger behind our break-up played out in the worse way. I worked hard to provide a loving and safe home for my children, and their father (in surreptitious) worked that much harder to destroy the relationship I had with them.

Secretly, he drilled into my daughter "I wasn't who she thought I was," he would tell her, "your mommy is this and she is that." Ultimately, he brainwashed her. He planted seeds in her that would in the end work against her. They began to surface when she was 13. Out of nowhere, she began to become as a thorn in my side. No matter how much I tried to give her love and support, it translated into me having an ulterior motive for doing what I did. I was now someone she could not believe in nor trust anymore; his plan had worked, he had discredited me in the eyes of my daughter. What I had taught her as good and right -before God, now in her mind, evil was good and right was evil.

She grew to become mean spirited; full of anger and outside of prayer, it seemed there was nothing I could do about it. When I finally realized what had happened to my beautiful baby girl, I was outraged. Although, I had to correct her behavior, I also recognized, I couldn't place all the blame on her.

However, my story concerning my daughter and our relationship doesn't end there. She would go own to be a wonderful person. But, it was through much intercession. It has been a long and hard journey. I am elated to report today she is an adult and my daughter is working hard to live a stronger healthier lifestyle both professionally and personally. She is also being intentional about having a better relationship with me, which by the way is growing stronger and stronger every day.

Justin was just like his mommy in a lot of ways. He was kind, compassionate, thoughtful and loving towards everyone. Justin never felt close to his dad, although he loved his dad very much. No matter how much love he received from mom, it was the love of his dad that he longed for. At the time of our break up their dad was young and I'm sure he loved his children. When I look back, I also realize he was blind-sighted to the long term affects his words and actions would have on our children's self-esteem.

Being a Christian and minister doesn't exclude us from having to deal with real, practical life issues. At thirteen, Justin began to complain that he was having a problem understanding his school work, I advocated for him to be evaluated. But, they didn't assess him, as I continuously suggested; they began to place labels on him. He is a "bad boy"-they said. I remember, in the first year of the seventh grade they placed him into an "alternative program". It was the affiliation with the boys in that program that introduced him to what became a long term struggle with drugs.

Here I am with a calling on my life to reach inner-city youth and raising a couple of them myself, but having challenges with my children. Every time I produced a play, I would pray that my children would catch the message and reach out to Christ. When you think in terms of counting the cost ...could my children's struggle be considered a cost? I had to really evaluate that thought. I had to look at the life of Job and Jesus. Considering Job's life, because in his time, he was an upright man before God, he lost everything; his land, his wealth and his children and even Jesus' life was given as a ransom for our lives.

If you knew Justin, you would have loved him... everyone did. He had an easy going personality and was thoughtful and respectful of others, always doing what he could to place a smile on your face. He didn't talk much, but when he did, it was with "deep thought". I remember how his smile lit up the room. I was not prepared for Justin's death. I always hoped that Justin would overcome his addiction and join me in the operations of the Recreation Center. Out of my three children, Justin cared for my work with the youth the most and now he was no longer here to share in, the joys of it with me.

On one occasion, Justin climbed into my bed one night, hallucinating because of taking a drug called "dipper". He awakened the next morning afraid in October of 2009, looked me in my eyes and said, "Mom! I need help!" After a few days, I realized I could not afford to put him in a private rehab, so I called the police and asked them to get him off the streets; the drug was altering his state of mind. Justin had petty charges but was not a convicted felon with a criminal record, he just needed help.

After about six weeks in jail, I was finally told he was going through a terrible detox. I spoke with the Jail's Mental Health Staff and begged them to help my son. They went before the Judge, got an order for Justin to be "restored". Justin was transferred off to a state institution. I had everyone praying for my son's life. I fasted and prayed and stood on the Word myself believing for a miracle.

After four months, I was told that he was doing great and would soon be coming home. One week before he was due to come home, my 22 year old son was strangled to death in his bed. As before mentioned, the phone rang 8:00 am, Sunday morning as I was preparing to leave for Church, I heard the fatality of my son. I remember sitting in the living room, hearing the muffled voices of family and friends. My mind flashing back over the years I had served God in ministry. As I stared into space, I heard my heart and my thoughts say...."why, why my son Lord?" In the quietness of that personal moment between me and God, stunned by the news, I heard God say, "Justin was a sacrificial lamb!"

It would be one year before I could embrace any part of what God said to me that day. At Justin's funeral one hundred youth and adults stood for up for salvation. Even, after Justin's death I didn't – I couldn't grieve. Many said, I was in denial and I guess I was, because I had convinced myself "woman of God" you can handle this. One year later, something else happened; and it flipped my life up-side down. At this point, I fell into a deep depression.

What is grief, and how can you know it, less you live through its ghastly grip? Everything in my life came to a screeching halt on that New Year's morning. I literally heard a deep dark whisper from outside of me say, "curse God and DIE!" My emotions were all over the place, I was weeping and crying with what I felt like a dagger sticking in my heart—my spirit trapped inside of my fleshly shell. I then heard the faint cry of my heart whisper, "help me"! At this point, my understanding of faith had no LOGIC. For the first time since my covenant with God at my desk, my relationship with God was in question. My desire to reach youth was no more and I wanted to curse God and DIE.

After about a week, I heard a faint whisper cry out again from my heart "help, me"! Suddenly, yet slowly, it was as if over the next six months, God's love and patience began to nurse me through the greatest fight of my life. Everything I had come to believe about God, His Word and His way, was being explored. I look back and ask the question, "What kept me connected to God at a point when many would have simply fallen apart and drifted away?" It was my intimate relationship I had with God. We talk about the importance of having a relationship with Jesus, but a healthy relationship involves at least two, each deeply committed to the other. In this moment in time, I realized I was beginning to get my fight back. God's love was always there, even when I embraced the negative emotions associated with grieving; anger, guilt, lack of faith, etcetera.

Over time, God gently, comforted me with the understanding associated with Justin's death as being settled in the cost. The dictionary's definition of cost is, "the price paid to acquire, produce, accomplish, or maintain anything." In my case, it would be anything for the Lord. I've heard it said that as we pray for our backslidden children, they are merely running around in the hand of God. Like the prodigal son, Justin had to come to the end of him self and completely surrender to God, which based on our last conversations, I know he did. *Except a corn of wheat fall into the ground and die, it abideth alone: but if it dies, it bringeth forth much fruit. John 12:24.*

I am at peace now with my son's life, I "paid the cost" of the Justin L. Davis Foundation and the vision to own a Christian Outreach Recreational Facility of the Arts. Moving forward, I can see the life of my son lived through every young man or woman rescued through this youth and young adult vision.

4 Tips to Get Your Fight Back – Through Tragedy

Turn to God – Regardless of your status, whether you are new in Christ; mature in Christ; a "prodigal" in Christ, one must admit their need for God. In times of crisis, we tend to turn away from him, but instead of doing that lets turn towards God.

Identify your motives – What is your intent for a relationship with God and what is God's intent for a relationship with you? Identify it! Since the human understanding is sometimes conceived out of years of dysfunctional role models (keeping in mind nobody but God is perfect); be willing to surrender to his purpose and process for your life…. In that -you will find peace.

Balance your emotions - Confess your true heart (vent to God); being honest with yourself and the Lord, is KEY. The balance is to fill your **mental bank** with "scriptural deposits" which creates a spiritual antenna that rises in times of crisis thus putting in perspective the dynamics that are in play. Will you be bitter or better! God allows time for us to grieve, but long-term depression is outside of God's will for our lives.

Wield your Sword – The sword being, the "Word of God" exercised through faith. It is now your time to "GET YOUR FIGHT BACK". Tame your tongue and position yourself, for your life is determined by it. Pick up your spiritual arsenal and aim for the enemy, using Declarations, Praise and Adoration to lift your spirit. Before you know it, you're on your way to full recovery and greater works for the Kingdom!

Define Your Money

Material Girl
by Elizabeth Felder

I t's Friday and she just got paid. About this time without fail appears the "*Material Girl*" in me and she's hungry to spend some money. Be careful, she can undermine every bit of progress she's made on the path to getting herself out of debt. Every day the mail man brings luscious catalogs filled with dresses, bags, shoes and diamonds. Every attempt at depriving or reasoning with the *"Material Girl in Me"* was fruitless. Money was my master and I was its slave.

I wonder are you just like me? After a long week of working you come home tired, having to feed the kids, help them with homework, and before you know it the clock says 10:00 pm. I believe that every *"Material Girl"* deserved to have a nice car, nice clothes, and of course that nice house. The *"Material Girl"* in me was so proud of all my possessions and of course, I needed to have space to store everything neatly, and specifically color coordinated. I even decided to take one of my extra bedrooms and turn it into a dressing room with custom cabinets, mirrors, and drawers. The *Material Girl* in me had it all, so I thought.

One Sunday after coming home from Church, I turned on the stove and started frying chicken for dinner. I went upstairs, as usual, to take off my Sunday clothes and all of a sudden I heard the smoke detector go off. I opened my bedroom door and the smoke had already filled the upper floor. I ran downstairs and saw the stove was on fire. I told my daughter to call the fire department. The grease had spilled over onto the top of the stove, which started a grease fire. I ran for the fire extinguisher and tried to put it out but, to no avail, the fire -- just kept growing bigger and bigger.

I could hear the fire engine siren coming near the house and driving away. I wondered why they were taking so long to get her to my house. Eventually, I was able to finally put the fire out, but the smoke was everywhere. I had to go outside and get some air. After what seems to be forever before the fire department finally arrived, I asked them what took them so long. The firemen said, "I couldn't find the house." Suddenly, I remembered that I hadn't closed the doors to any of the upstairs rooms- oh, my God!

Well, I know you know what happened. The very thing I had loved the most and spent all my money on was now black and smelled like smoke. The beautiful walk-in closet was filled with smoke and soot from the fire. Not only were the clothes ruined, but I purchased almost everything on credit. I now had a $12,000 debt I had to pay back with nothing to show for it.

That's when I knew that the, *"Material Girl"* in me had to die. Are you or do you know of any *"Material Girls'*? Tell them to read this story to learn how to stop her in her tracks with this Action Plan.

How to Eliminate Emotional Spending

Why spend money on what is not bread, and your labor on what does not satisfy? (Isa.55:2)

I must confess that I was addicted to spending and using my credit card. I learned the hard way that emotional spending is simply a pacifier to inner issues that were bothering me. I used sales and coupons as an anesthetic, but I never had the required surgery in order to become healthy.

The average person indulges in emotional spending habits -- mainly as a way to:

- Cope with stress,
- Cure the blues,
- Diffuse feelings of anger or frustration,
- Ease boredom,
- Feel special, and
- Soothe ourselves after a bad day (or reward ourselves for a good one),

H.A.L.T

Consider the word HALT which stands for "**H**ungry, **A**ngry, **L**onely and **T**ired." When we are in a state of hunger, anger, loneliness or tiredness, we make poor choices and more vulnerable to temptation, we are in a physiological state of stress. When we are stressed we interact in self-defeating or alienating ways. When you're feeling any of these four emotions, you should avoid shopping because it leads to bad spending decisions. The key is to deal directly with whatever is making you unhappy instead of spending money to feel better.

Now let's talk about ways to fight the desire, or urge to spend, spend, spend….

4 Tips to Get Your Fight Back – Emotional Spending

Notice the feelings. This is the process of acknowledging your feelings and making a quality decision to change. You must pay attention to what is propelling you to spend, whether it's the need to erase the fallout from a fight or to celebrate after a hard day.

Find Alternative Activities. Do you love to use shopping as a form of entertainment, or take your mind off your problems? Take the time to identify what you're feeling when you want to buy something and choose a more constructive behavior that will help you deal with that emotion.

Limit your Exposure to Temptation. Take steps to intentionally limit your exposure to whatever it is that makes you want to spend. Don't watch the Shopping Networks on cable. If it is not in your budget and not a need, then don't buy it now.

Make Yourself Accountable. Another powerful strategy is to find ways to hold yourself accountable for your actions. Ask the people you live with you or those you spend the most time with to help you by making you aware of what you are about to do.

Before You Say "I Do"!
by Elizabeth Felder

J ust imagine yourself wearing a blindfold over your eyes walking aimlessly on the roof of a 30-story building. As you begin to feel your way around looking for the edge, you jump off and plunge head first unto the cold hard pavement. I don't know about you, but that would be true suicide. What am I talking about here? Whether you may believe this or not, this is how most women go into their marriage. They are wearing an invisible blindfold over their eyes with their intended spouse as they stumbled and feel their way to the altar.

In June of 2008, I received a call from my very best girl friend Carol. We had been friends since we were twelve. I loved spending the weekends at her house. We would go into her mother's old cedar chest and carefully un-wrap her mother's wedding gown. She would put the cream dress on and I would always help her with the many buttons that rested neatly down the back of the long beautiful dress. She pretended to be the bride and I was her maid of honor. One day, we made a promise to each other; regardless of where we lived, close or far, we would be each other's maid of honor.

In June of 2008, when I received that call from Carol, I knew that the time had come for one of us to fulfill the promise of being her Maid-Of-Honor. My best friend was getting married to the man of her dreams. I asked her how long she knew him and she said, "only six months". Of course a red flag went off in my mind, but I couldn't spoil it for her, so I let it go that day. Every now and then I would ask questions about her prince, but she would always change the subject as though she really didn't know the answers. All she talked about was how happy she was to finally be getting married and she looked forward to having children, just as I had several years before.

I had never been a maid of honor before and had no ideal the amount of preparation involved in the process. I spent several months with her planning the wedding ceremony. I wanted to make sure that everything went perfect on that special day for her. After she gave me the exact wedding date, we then discussed who would be in the wedding, where it would be held, and who would perform the ceremony. We created the guest list, arrangements for the minister, and ordered the wedding invitations and flowers.

Late one night I received a call from Carol, she was crying so hard I couldn't understand a word that she was saying. After about 10 minutes of noise, she finally was able to get out the words that she didn't have the additional $10,000.00 dollars needed to pay the caterer nor the church and limousine fees.

Carol said "her fiancé had lost his job several months before and that he didn't have any money to help with the expenses." I told Carol I would be right over and we would find a way to get the additional money needed for her big day.

When I arrived at Carol's apartment, her prince was just sitting on the sofa eating a slice of pizza and watching a basketball game. He wasn't concerned about the emotional state that Carol was in nor did he even say hello upon me entering the living room. I told Carol to get her coat and let's take a drive, so that she could clear her head and put a plan in action.

Never marry a man who can't share
with you the amount of money he makes.

We drove to a diner and sat down to have a cup of coffee and a slice of cheesecake. I told Carol that I really wanted her to be honest with me about what was really going on between her and prince charming. Since I was a coach, I had to really put aside our friendship and ask some serious questions that might cause our relationship to change over night. As I shared with her some of my personal experiences, in my own marriage she began to open up. I pulled out a piece of paper and a pen and asked her several questions that would bring light to her financial situation and pending marriage. I asked her how did she meet her prince, where did he worked, what was his salary, did she meet his family or even know any of his friends and the list went on. As we worked through each question, she began to cry again, because now she had come to the full realization that her walk down the altar would not happen. She had made the mistake that so many of women make which is rushing to the altar without first preparing the foundation for a lasting marriage. I have found that 48% of marriages end in divorce because of money. It is based on what the wife didn't find out about her husband "before" they were married. If you feel that finances WILL be an issue then you should consider counseling or worse case, reconsider the marriage. The financial situation won't be any better if you have to spend thousands of dollars dissolving a marriage.

Below are 10 questions that every woman must have the answer to before she says, "I Do".

10 Tips to Get Your Fight Back – Steps Before Marriage

Know His Character. Before you say I do, get to know the man on the inside. He may look good, smell good and feel good, but what type of man is he, really? Is he kind and patient? Does he take care of his mother, handle his bills well, can you trust him, and is he a man of honor, etcetera.

Know His Salary. Many women have made the mistake of taking the man's word as to what his salary is, but you better get some proof (show me the paycheck). Where does he work, how much does he bring home, where is the money going, and is he paying child support? When financial issues arise in the home and bill collectors are ringing your phone, romance will go out the window. There is a saying: "No Finance = No Romance"

Know His Job History. Never marry a man who DOES NOT HAVE A JOB ladies. Ask him about his job history. How long has he been on his present and past jobs? If he has a history of changing/or getting fired from a job every six months, then you might have a problem here. What are his career plans? Do they make sense? Here's a big one: is he self-employed? Will he bring home a constant paycheck or just hits now and then?

Know His Credit Score. Think about it, you both dream of owing a house or buying a car together. One day you go to get a mortgage and you are turned down. That's when you find out that he never pays his bills on time, he has outstanding loans, and he has his name on other houses and cars.

Know Your Joint Financial Obligations. Ladies when you marry your spouse you legally become obligated to pay his bills. You cannot marry him without marrying either his asset's or his liabilities. Your not legally obligated to pay debts that were created before the marriage, but the money the he uses to pay those bills are now apart of your household income or debt.

Know His Actions. Pay close attention when in the dating stages of the relationship. Observe how your partner spends, saves, or uses his money. Watch for the red flags.

Know His Communication Skills. Can he talk comfortably about his finances and disclose his salary, spending habits, and savings to you? If he becomes uncomfortable and tries to change the subject concerning finances -- then that's another red flag.

Know Who Will Handle the Bills. Discuss who is going to handle paying the bills. Both of you need to be fully aware of ALL the bills and every penny that is coming in and going out. On the flip side, be aware of a spouse who wants complete control and doesn't want you to "worry about a thing." This may be a sign of Financial Control Issues. At first it sounds wonderful, but Wedding Girl Beware.

Know His Philosophies About Money. Marriage counselors will tell you not to marry someone expecting to change them. In addition, opposites may attract in many ways, but when it comes to finances, that isn't generally true. A married hardcore saver and hardcore spender will quickly realize that they've got serious issues.

Are You Financially Compatible.   You can see if you're compatible by doing a 30 day trial budget and see what happens.

Know His/Her Financial Goals.   Talk about where both of you want to be, financially in 10, 20 or 30 years. Does he want to have kids and how many because kids cost MONEY? Does he like clothes and fancy cars? Or is he a saver and wants a home of his own, planning for future goals such as retirement, school, vacations. How does he treat his mother when it comes to money? Does he buy you cheap gifts on holidays?

Seven Habits of Financially Successful Women
by Elizabeth Felder

T his section will help you become motivated, but making it a habit is what will keep you going. Studies have shown that practically any habit can be established in a 90— day period. A routine can be tough, because as humans, we are inheritably lazy and it is easier to talk the talk, but not walk the walk. Your present state of mind says it's easy to maintain because it is comfortable and is the path of least resistance. Webster's Dictionary defines a habit as, "An acquired mode of behavior that has become nearly or completely involuntary." It takes approximately 90 days to condition yourself to create (or break) a habit. Once it is created, those actions happen with little or no conscious processes.

Remember when you first started driving a car, and how you constantly had to think about each procedure. You had to put the belt on, check the mirrors, turn on the ignition, check your surroundings, apply the break, and shift into gear, etcetera. As time goes on, you became more confident and were driving places while talking on the phone, listening to music, drinking coffee, and not even consciously remembering how you got to your destination. Habits like these are either helping or preventing you from reaching your goals.

So here is what you will have to do. Each day read a Wealth Habit Section. After you read the section take a dollar bill ($1.00) and place it in an envelope. After your first seven (7) days you should have seven dollars ($7.00) in the envelope. You must repeat this step several times. At the end of the 90 days you will have $90.00 in your envelope. The next seven (7) days you are required to wake up early and give God praise for the new wealth that you are receiving now and will receive in days to come. Take this money and open a savings account or sow a seed at your local church. This Wealth Habit will be the starting point for your inner healing as well as the road to getting out of debt.

Tips to Get Your Fight Back – 6 Habits of Financially Success Women

Create A Wealthy Vision:, Mindset, and goals are the manifestation of your vision.

Create A Spending Plan: Get organized, remove the clutter.

Form an Emergency Fund: Use cash instead of charge cards for emergencies.

Get Out Of DEBT: "Detox" your debt and use cash as King.

Become A Producer and Not a Consumer (a) invest (b) savings (c) buy assets (d) start a business (e) create multiple streams of income.

Protect Your Wealth: Follow the plan and put everything in writing in a safe place.

Pass On Generational Wealth. Don't let all your hard work go in vain. Pass it on to the next generation.

The "Get Your Fight Back" System

Get inspired, raise your self esteem and discover your
unlimited potential with the
"Girl, Get Your Fight Back" System.
This is not a course, but a life changing experience
which will take you on an inward journey after which
you will never be the same.

Seven Step "Get Your Fight Back" Plan

The *Seven Step "Girl, Get Your Fight Back Program"* provides a solid foundation for recovering from a set back in life.

1.   **Look At It:** Take a good look at the situation and assess the problem. How did it start, who were the players and how did it end?

2.   **Kill It:** It is important that you accept responsibility for your setback. Take a good look in the mirror -- did you contribute to the problem or not? When you accept responsibility, you are giving yourself the power to make the necessary changes to remedy the situation and not repeat it.

3.   **Clean Yourself Up:** Take care of yourself. Take care of your wounds, dry your tears and shake it off. **Don't beat yourself up.** Handle your emotions and get support – if you need to vent – its o.k.

4.   **Make a Plan:** To achieve victory, a specific strategy needs to be in place and then applied. You must decide what

you're going to do about this setback, focus on a clear solution, and the needed steps to prevent it from happening again.

Here Are The 4 Main Steps To Take:

(1) Create a Vision,
(2) Make a Decision,
(3) Take Action, and
(4) Desire = Power.
(Note: a decision without action is simply an illusion.)

5.   **Change Your Mindset then Your Talk**: You will never stay free until you change the way you think. When you change your talk you can then change your walk. It will cost you something, but you will win if you faint not. What you think about will come about.

6.   **Reposition Yourself**. Take a look at your surroundings. You will need to make a **DECISION** to change yourself, your friends or location? The word *decision* is Greek, "to cut". When you make an incision you are cutting into something. When you make a decision you cut "off!" something. This is where you take the responsibility to cut off people, places, and things that will hinder your progress.

7.   **Fuel Your Desire:** Your desire is the energy you're willing to exert in order to reach your goal. How bad do you want success? What are you willing to do to achieve your goals?

Know the best is yet to come. Now its time to have faith and remind yourself you are blessed and highly favored. Everyone has setbacks, but you must remember that a setback is your ladder to a comeback. No, stand up and keep moving forward. Setbacks and weaknesses can be robust stepping stones that lead to growth and maturity. *Rebuild, Rediscover, and Renew Yourself.* **Always try to focus on the successes you have already achieved and it will grow and expand in your life.**

Be persistent and turn a setback into an opportunity to solidify your real confidence. Regardless of what happens, you can handle it. Regardless of how your body feels, you'll move through the anxiety and come out the other side smiling.

Remember it's a "Minor *Setback* for a Major Comeback."

"Weight Loss" Get Your Fight Back Plan

Making lifestyle changes to lose weight isn't easy, especially when you have lived with unhealthy eating habits all your life. Anytime you make plans to lose weight their will always be challenges you will have to face called side-steps or set-backs. It is really easy to slip back into your old eating habits. The most important thing you must do is to have a plan in place when these set-backs happen. Here are simple steps you can implement to land back on your feet:

- **Create a Plan**. This doesn't mean that you plan to fail, but rather set in motion a plan for success. Be honest about your setbacks, such as depression, stress, being over worked or maybe you're an emotional eater. Identify set-back triggers and then try to avoid them.

- **Forgive Yourself**. If you do have a set-back, don't sit around having a pity party or a blaming session. Take a look at what happened, make a change and then move on with your plan.

- **Avoid Temptations**. Until you are strong, don't place yourself in situations that might tempt you. Avoid junk food at all costs, which will minimize the chances of a setback.

- **Exercise and Drink Water**. In order to loss the weight and avoid weight loss setbacks you must exercise which will kick start your metabolism. Most important, drink plenty of water. Just remember that water is your best friend during weight loss

Get Your Fight Back "After A Breakup" Plan

B reakups are truly rough, no one really wants to experience the hurt that comes with a set back in regards to relations. Below are a few helpful tips about how to make it a little easier.

1. **<u>Letting Go</u>**. When any type of relationship ends, whether it was your choice or not, you must practice letting go and allowing the healing process to begin. Trust and know that everything happens for a reason and this is the best thing for you right now. The reasons will eventually become clear as you begin to heal.

2. **<u>Release your tension and any bundled up anxiety</u>**. Begin to talk with friends you can trust and confide in. You can even punch a pillow, scream out loud or even cry. Don't turn your conversation or tears into a pity party that you want your friends to join in.

3. **<u>Love Yourself</u>**. One of the best healers is the practice of loving yourself. Loving yourself will guide you on the road to happiness and emotional stability.

4. **Don't rethink your decision**. Try not to second-guess your decision. Follow your inner voice deep within. It will not steer you wrong. Don't convince yourself that maybe he wasn't so bad or you just need to hold on because you think that someone else will get him.

5. **Stay away from your ex**. Don't keep seeing each other, stop calling, e-mailing, or texting your ex. When you are trying to move on it is always best to stay apart as much as possible so that you can allow yourself to become single, in your mind, body and soul.

6. **Deal with the hate phase**. Yes, it's ok to feel hate, disappointment, angry and the like. This is the phase you want to move through quickly and it can easily turn into more than just anger. It's truly a waste of time or energy to tear yourself apart over something you no longer have power over.

7. **Make a list of the reasons you made your decision.** The best way to help you stick to your decision is to make a list of why you came to this decision. When you write all your observation on paper, you are painting a picture that you can use for your emotions to heal.

8. **Breaking can signify a new beginning**. This is an excellent time to organize your space, do some cleaning, and get rid of any memories. This will leave you feeling refreshed, as well as, prepare you for the new things to

come. Get ride of those memory triggers. These are all the things that remind you of your ex - a smell, a song, or even a place. You can do those things again after you have healed- if need be.

9. **<u>Find happiness through other things in your life</u>**. There is light at the end of tunnel. Join a club, sign up for classes, go out with friends. The best revenge is not looking back, but moving forward. Enjoy being single again. There are so many things that singles can do that couples can't.

Get Your Fight Back "Start Your Own Business" Plan

by Elizabeth Felder

As we always say, plan your life, then plan your business. Some of the most successful and happy people we know are entrepreneurs who created a business that's in perfect synchronicity with what they want out of life. If you do what you love, you'll work harder, better and more happily.

Below are the major steps you must take to be successful:

1. Create A Life Plan
2. Do your research first and foremost
3. Visit the Small Business Administration (SCORE)
4. Decide which business is right for your personality, lifestyle and income goals
5. Decide on a Business Structure
6. Name Your Business
7. Obtain your business license
8. Get your federal tax ID number
9. Obtain a sales license if needed
10. Find Great People (Mentors, Networking)
11. Establish a Brand (Niche)
12. Market, Market, Market and Sell

Low Cost Businesses You Can Start NOW

The most obvious reason to pursue low cost business opportunities is that you can do it easily and quickly. You don't have to get a business plan approved for a bank loan, you don't have to explain to Uncle Ed how you'll repay him, and you don't have to take a second mortgage or raid the college savings.

In other words, low cost business opportunities typically grant you greater financial freedom and flexibility since you're not tying up as much cash. A couple of small business ideas with flexibility...

Bookkeeping
Consulting
Manufacturer's rep
Security specialist
Transcription service

Business support
Desktop publishing
Medical claims
Seminar production
Virtual assistant business

Creative Ideas
Arts & crafts business
Interior designer

Creativity consultant
Jewelry

Doing What You Love
Freelancing your expertise
Sports business

Hobby business
Personal Services

Child-care	Elder Care
Financial Advisor	Organizer
Personal concierge	Personal shopper
Remodeling contractor	Tutoring service
Wedding consultant	

Other Services

Cleaning	Event planning
Mobile photography	Product Sales
Cart/kiosk	Direct sales
eBay	Gift basket

Even More Ideas

Senior care ideas   Senior day-care center, Relocation service for home downsizing, Home care and home, health-care services, personal assistance, Transportation service

Pet businesses   Pet Photography, Dog Clothing and Accessories, Pet Sitting, Dog Walker, Dog Obedience Training

Part-time business ideas   Antiques, Computer Tutor, Custom Jewelry and Accessories, Espresso Cart, Garage and Attic Cleaning/Hauling Service, Medical Transcription, Office and Home Organizer, Personal Trainer, Records Search, Yoga and Tai Chi Instructor, Line Dance Instructor

Service businesses   Mobile Pet Grooming, Diaper Delivery, Dry-Cleaning Pickup & Delivery, Mobile Massage, Seamstress/Tailor, Court-Paper Serving, Cover Letter/Resume Service, Event Planner, Mystery Shopping, Professional Organizer, Tutor,

Weekend businesses ideas   Holistic Housecleaning, Christmas Light Installer or House Stagers.

Get Your Fight Back Journal

What is a journal? This journal is a daily account of your life as it pertains to the relationship with yourself, relationship with others and your relationship of how you use your money. Keeping a journal is not the same as keeping a diary. A diary records events as they happen, usually on a daily basis. A journal is a record of thoughts, feelings and memories over a longer period of time. This way, over the weeks, months and years you will see patterns, notice changes and progress, and monitor your growth.

This journal is broken down into three (3) sections:

1. The relationship with yourself,
2. The relationship with others around you; and
3. Your relationship of how you use your money.

So now let's begin your healing and turning a set-back into a come-back.

Fight Back Journal -
Your Relationship with Yourself

Who are you? What do you look like?
How do you feel about yourself? Do you like the way you look?
Do you love yourself? (Write about yourself)

_____

_____

_____

What experience have you gone through that set you back?

_____

_____

_____

What steps must you take to get your fight back?

_____

_____

_____

Are there any other things that you have uncovered about
yourself?

_____

_____

_____

Fight Back Journal - Your Relationship with Others

Who are your friends, family, and co-workers? How do you interact with them? Are these healthy relationships? Who are the people you need to disconnect from? Who and where are the people you need to connect with?

_____

_____

_____

What experience have you gone through that set you back?

_____

_____

_____

What steps must you take to get your fight back?

_____

_____

_____

Are there any other things that you have uncovered about these connections?

_____

_____

_____

Fight Back Journal -
Your Relationship with Money

Are you living a prosperous life? Are you in debt? Do you have anything to show for all the money that you have spent?   Are living from paycheck to paycheck? Do you need to improve your credit score?   Are you eating out or buying too many shoes, clothes, etc?   (Be honest with yourself, its ok.)

_____

_____

_____

What experience have you gone through that set you back?

_____

_____

_____

What steps must you take to get your fight back?

_____

_____

_____

Get Your Fight Back Quotes from Famous Women

1. "Life is a succession of lessons which must be lived to be understood." *~ Helen Keller, American Author and Activist*

2. "I may be compelled to face danger, but never fear it, and while our soldiers can stand and fight, I can stand and feed and nurse them." *~ Clara Barton, Founder of the American Red Cross*

3. "When you get into a tight place and everything goes against you, till it seems as though you could not hang on a minute longer, never give up then, for that is just the place and time that the tide will turn. " *~ Harriet Beecher Stowe, American Abolitionist and Author*

4. "If you have made mistakes, there is always another chance for you. You may have a fresh start any moment you choose, for this thing we call 'failure' is not the falling down, but the staying down." *~ Mary Pickford, Canadian-born Actress, co-founder of United Artists*

5. "Life is very interesting. In the end, some of your greatest pains become your greatest strengths." *~ Drew Barrymore, American Actress*

6. "The greatest part of our happiness depends on our dispositions, not our circumstances." *~ Martha Washington, First Lady of the United States*

7. "You must do the thing you think you cannot do." *~ Eleanor Roosevelt, First Lady of the United States from 1933-1945*

Get Your Fight Back Quotes from Great Men

1. "Put yourself in a state of mind where you say to yourself, 'Here is an opportunity for me to celebrate like never before; my own power, my own ability to get myself to do whatever is necessary'." ~ **Dr. Martin Luther King, American Clergyman and Leader of Civil Rights Movement**

2. "I cried aloud to the LORD, and he answered me from his holy hill. Selah" ~ **David, King of Israel & Judah**

3. "It is said an Eastern monarch once charged his wise men to invent him a sentence to be ever in view, and which should be true and appropriate in all times and situations. They presented him the words: 'And this, too, shall pass away'." ~ **Abraham Lincoln, 19th President of the United States of America**

4. "The pessimist sees difficulty in every opportunity. The optimist sees opportunity in every difficulty" ~ **Winston Churchill, Prime Minister of England during WWII**

5. "... Tie a knot and hang on" "When you come to the end of your rope, tie a knot and hang on. " ~ **Franklin D. Roosevelt, 37th, 38th, 39th and 40th President of the United States of America**

6. "When written in Chinese the word "crisis" is composed of two characters one represents danger and the other represents opportunity." ~ **John F. Kennedy, 44th President of the United States of America**

7. "There are those who look at things the way they are, and ask why... I dream of things that never were, and ask why not?" ~ **Robert "Bobby" Kennedy, American Politician and Civil Right Activist**

8. "If you hear voices within you say "you cannot paint," then by all means paint and that voice will be silenced." ~ **Vincent Van Gogh, Dutch Painter**

9. "When one door closes another door opens; but we so often look so long and so regretfully upon the closed door, that we do not see the ones which open for us." ~ **Alexander Graham Bell, Scottish Scientist and Inventor**

10. "When everything seems to be going against you, remember that the airplane takes off against the wind, not with it." ~ **Henry Ford, American Industrialist, Founder of Ford Motor Company**

11. "I'd rather be a could-be if I cannot be an are; because a could-be is a maybe who is reaching for a star, I'd rather be a has-been than a might-have-been, by far; for a might have-been has never been, but a has- was once an are." ~ **Milton Berle, American Comedian and Actor**

12. "It's not whether you get knocked down. It's whether you get up again." ~ **Vince Lombardi, American Football Coach**

Scripture Get Your Fight Back Quotes

1. ***Deuteronomy 31:6*** Be strong and courageous. Do not fear or be in dread of them, for it is the LORD your God who goes with you. He will not leave you or forsake you."

2. ***Isaiah 41:10*** fear not, for I am with you; be not dismayed, for I am your God; I will strengthen you, I will help you, I will uphold you with my righteous right hand.

3. ***Zephaniah 3:17*** The LORD your God is in your midst, a mighty one who will save; he will rejoice over you with gladness; he will quiet you by his love; he will exult over you with loud singing.

4. ***1 Corinthians 10:13*** No temptation has overtaken you that is not common to man. God is faithful, and he will not let you be tempted beyond your ability, but with the temptation he will also provide the way of escape, that you may be able to endure it.

5. ***2 Corinthians 4:16-18*** *So,* we do not lose heart. Though our outer self is wasting away, our inner self is being renewed day by day. For this light momentary affliction is preparing for us an eternal weight of glory beyond all comparison, as we look not to the things that are seen but to the things that are unseen. For the things that are seen are transient, but the things that are unseen are eternal.

Comfort and Encouragement Bible Verses

6. ***Deuteronomy 31:8*** *It is the LORD who goes before you. He will be with you; he will not leave you or forsake you. Do not fear or be dismayed."*

7. ***Psalm 9:9*** The LORD is a stronghold for the oppressed, a stronghold in times of trouble. And those who know your name put their trust in you, for you, O LORD, have not forsaken those who seek you.

8. **Psalm 23:4** Even though I walk through the valley of the shadow of death, I will fear no evil, for you are with me; your rod and your staff, they comfort me.

9. **Psalm 55:22** Cast your burden on the LORD, and he will sustain you; he will never permit the righteous to be moved.

10. **Matthew 11:28-29** Come to me, all who labor and are heavy laden, and I will give you rest. Take my yoke upon you, and learn from me, for I am gentle and lowly in heart, and you will find rest for your souls.

Peace Scripture Quotes for Encouragement

11. **John 14:27** *Peace I leave with you; my peace I give to you. Not as the world gives do I give to you. Let not your hearts be troubled, neither let them be afraid.*

12. **John 16:33** I have said these things to you, that in me you may have peace. In the world you will have tribulation. But take heart; I have overcome the world."

13. **Romans 8:6** For to set the mind on the flesh is death, but to set the mind on the Spirit is life and peace.

14. **Philippians 4:6-7** do not be anxious about anything, but in everything by prayer and supplication with thanksgiving let your requests be made known to God. And the peace of God, which surpasses all understanding, will guard your hearts and your minds in Christ Jesus.

15. **Colossians 3:15** And let the peace of Christ rule in your hearts, to which indeed you were called in one body. And be thankful.

Meet the Authors

Tamara Elizabeth
www.Moximize.me

Tamara Elizabeth is a certified self-love coach and Master Motivator of women in transition. She is the author of an inspirational workbook titled, *Fabulously Fifty and Reflecting It! –Discovering My Lovable Me.*

Tamara Elizabeth was born in Vancouver, British Columbia, Canada. She was raised by American parents in a Canadian culture and lives both traditions with pride. She has worn many hats; daughter, wife, mother, fund-raiser, school builder, space challenger, and travel photographer.

Lezlyn Parker
www.Fightback500.info

Lezlyn Parker is a relationship architect, life coach and a Mary Kay consultant. She and her husband, Johnny, are founders of The Parker Group, LLC where they teach and empower couples to build relationships that flourish. Mrs. Parker has spoken nationally for over 10 years with Family Life's "Weekend to Remember" marriage conferences with her husband. She enjoys reading, traveling, and hanging out with her husband and three sons; JP, Jordan, and Joel and their energetic Cocker spaniel Jay-Jay.

Mrs. Parker has a B.A. in Elementary Education from Liberty University. She and her family reside outside of Washington, D.C.

Rosalind Y. Tompkins
www.UnlockingBeautyFromWithin.com

Rosalind Y. Tompkins is the published author of the books, "As Long As There Is Breath In Your Body, There Is Hope", "Rare Anointing", and "You Are Beautiful." With over twenty-years in recovery, former addict founded Mothers In Crisis, Inc., in 1991 and Turning Point International Church in 1998, where she currently serves as the senior pastor. Rosalind Y. Tompkins is a Freedom Maker, who connects with others in order to strengthen and add value to individuals, collective assignments, mandates for purpose and destiny to be revealed and fulfilled.

Sandra J. Bradley
www.BasketsBySandra.com

Sandra J. Bradley is a small business owner of "Baskets by Sandra." She resides in Norfolk, Virginia and she is the founder of Living Water Ministries. Her desire is for God to allow her to tell her story to others. Also, her prayer is that her transparency in her story will inspire others.

She is currently in seminary obtaining her Masters Degree. She is a wife, a mother two and a grandmother of three beautiful little girls. Her motto is *"Never give up. God will carry you when you can't carry yourself."* Sandra is currently working on her first book.

Mary Davisson
www.WellofWater.com

Mary Davisson

Mary Davisson currently attends Washington Bible College and is an ordained minister, a published author, business advisor, coach, manager, image consultant, accountant, mother, entrepreneur, and a force to be reckoned with. She has a passion for others to navigate life effectively, to discern when to seize life altering moments, when to connect the dots, and when to make the right connections.

Mary is tremendously meritorious from teaching, preaching, speaking, administration, to serving the body of Christ efficiently. This woman's style, contagious spirit, and her ability to reach others and to see God's power active in their life is the primary foundation for why Mary does what she does.

Courtney Artiste

www.FullyPersuadedem.com

Courtney Bowers-Artiste is the wife of Gary Artiste and the mother of 5 children. She is a published author and is the CEO of T.N.T. Establishments LLC, which is comprised of several businesses. She has committed her life to taking the message of God's faithfulness to the masses. Her calling is to enlighten, encourage and empower.

Courtney has her own unique contemporary style and an extreme passion for the people and things of God. She speaks with authority, simplicity, and boldness. She is currently working towards her bachelor's degree from the Cornerstone School of Theology.

Denise Wilkins
www.JustinlDavisFoundation.org

Denise Wilkins

Denise Wilkins has three grown children, the youngest deceased and seven grandchildren with a host of spiritual children, grandchildren and godchildren. She is a respected Evangelist/Minister, Counselor, Motivational Speaker, Theatrical Arts Writer, Director and Producer.

Her latest production, "Black Lights Shining in the Darkness" reached over 2,000 youth and adults with the Gospel. She wants the world to know, that after great suffering, you will discover God's JOY!

Elizabeth Felder

www.WomenWhoWin.us

A native of Long Island, New York, Elizabeth Felder is regarded as one of the most powerful and engaging professional speakers on the speaking circuit today. Elizabeth Felder is an Author, Certified Human Behavior Specialist, and Success Coach.

In 2005, Elizabeth launched UnStoppable, LLC, a full-service empowerment firm providing financial literacy and empowerment training. In addition, Elizabeth founded the UnStoppable Women & Teens, an organization that helps low income youth and women learn to rebuild their lives and empower them for greatness.

As a speaker, Elizabeth readily draws upon her extensive experience from over 20 years in corporate law, real estate, and entrepreneurship. She is an over-comer of the adversity of domestic abuse, abandonment, bankruptcy, divorce and homelessness.

Elizabeth is also the highly acclaimed author of two books, including her best seller, UnStoppable Teen Power and UnStoppable Wealthy Women. Her books motivate and educate people to realize their own potential to achieve greatness.

Quite simply, Elizabeth Felder is recognized nationwide by meeting planners and coordinators to be their Speaker of the Year for 2008.

Elizabeth says' that, "Before the foundations of the earth, I was ordained that I would empower, encourage, and exhort both Christians and non-Christians to live a full and abundant life". Her purpose is to teach people how to develop and enhance their life and their relationship with others. She is now committed to helping others move into their destiny and achieve there dreams. She wants you to know that your set-back is only getting you ready for a come-back.

Available to Speak At Your Next Event

Availability:
Available to speak at schools, churches, colleges, non-profits, women's groups, prisons, self-help groups, etc.

Speaking Fee/Honorarium:
Call for quote. Discounts given to non-profits

Media Interviews:
Call for details.

Contact:
(866) 940-2941
Media Department
Email - WomenWhoWin@live.com

Join us in our Mission to Push into Destiny 100,000 Women

At Women Who Win, LLC we believe that all women have an innate wisdom that is meant to be shared. The Women Who Win Series is an inspirational series of books and anthologies featuring the stores of women just like YOU! Real Women, Real Stores.

Have you joined the Women Who Win Network? If you haven't now is a great time to visit us on the web at www.WomenWhoWin.us. Ask all your friends to join too and help bring us closer to our goal of reaching 100,000 Women!

Yours truly,

Coach Elizabeth

Website: www.WomenWhoWin.us

Email: womenwhowin@live.com

ISBN-13: 978-1468128178 | ISBN-10: 1468128175

Made in the USA
Charleston, SC
31 January 2012